PROJECTING ENVIRONMENTAL TRENDS FROM
ECONOMIC FORECASTS

Projecting Environmental Trends from Economic Forecasts

PETER B. MEYER
THOMAS S. LYONS
TARA L. CLAPP
Center for Environmental Policy and Management,
College of Business and Public Administration,
University of Louisville

Ashgate

Aldershot • Burlington USA • Singapore • Sydney

Published by
Ashgate Publishing Ltd
Gower House
Croft Road
Aldershot
Hants GU11 3HR
England

Ashgate Publishing Company
131 Main Street
Burlington
Vermont 05401
USA

Ashgate website: http://www.ashgate.com

British Library Cataloguing in Publication Data
Meyer, Peter B.
  Projecting environmental trends from economic forecasts. -
  (Ashgate studies in environmental policy and practice)
  1. Economic forecasting 2. Environmental economics
  I. Title II. Lyons, Thomas S. III. Clapp, Tara L.
  333.7

Library of Congress Control Number: 00-133522

ISBN 1 84014 194 8

Printed and bound by Athenaeum Press, Ltd.,
Gateshead, Tyne & Wear.

Contents

List of figures and tables

Acknowledgments

Financial support for the study on which this volume is based was provided through a grant from the Regional and State Planning Division, Office of Program Planning and Evaluation, U.S. Environmental Protection Agency to the Kentucky Long Term Policy Research Center. Michael Childress, the Executive Director of the Center, recruited us for the project and offered essential direction, assistance and support. The University of Louisville and its Kentucky Institute for the Environment and Sustainable Development provided further funds and support, expanding the scope of the project.

The Tellus Institute in Boston provided us with the Stockholm Environment Institute's POLESTAR program for environmental forecasting, along with excellent support from Steve Bernow and Charlie Heaps. In Kentucky, Nancy Fouser of the Natural Resources and Environmental Protection Cabinet worked tirelessly to find us data, while Perry Nutt of the Legislative Research Commission manipulated the state's econometric forecasting model, helping to quantify our projections.

Steve Keach of the U.S. EPA provided resource materials from other relevant activities of the EPA. Our colleagues in the Kentucky Institute for the Environment and Sustainable Development offered additional data and served as reality testers for our projections and forecasts. We are especially indebted to Alan Dittmer, Russ Prough, Hugh Spencer, Jan Stevenson and David Wicks, who assisted us with the conduct of the advisory group sessions that helped to focus the project. The forty-odd participants in these sessions shaped the whole project.

For assistance with the preparation of this book, we would like to thank Angela Keene and Stefanie Shull. Sarah Markham of Ashgate Publishing gave her patient and professional support to the completion of this volume.

With thanks to all, we offer our findings. Despite our overwhelming debts to so many others, we alone are responsible for these conclusions.

1 Forecasting for sustainability

The purpose of this book is to outline a forecasting method targeted at changing current policy in the direction of sustainability; a method that bridges the gap between the goal of sustainable development and the barriers faced in the implementation of sustainable development. The forecasting techniques can be used to estimate the environmental impacts of economic policy choices in the medium term; the evaluation of current possible alternative paths is the most achievable forecasting goal. The mix of techniques we illustrate, and the attention to barriers to acceptance and implementation, are central to producing information with the potential to influence current choices towards more environmentally sustainable economic policies.

The concept of sustainable development is gaining currency in many, if not most, policy contexts. The concept of sustainable development emphasizes a balanced relationship between ecology, economy and social life, for current and future generations. Since its introduction by the Brundtland Commission (WCED 1987), in its broad outlines sustainable development has become an accepted vision of a development outcome. The implication of a sustainable development vision implies that choices in any one area require the assessment of consequences in the others.

However, in many political contexts there are many barriers to planning for sustainability. First of all, there are differences, some of which are quite deep, in concepts of the defining conditions of sustainable development. These differences are akin to different views of a "good life," or a "good society." Policy is made on some middle ground of current accepted views held by policy makers and politicians (Fiorino 1995). Sustainable development offers a vision of the future; a normative goal against which we can compare the many possible undesirable futures. The acceptable means by which sustainable development might be achieved are dependent on the

1

capacity for concerted and integrated actions, the legitimacy of public intervention, ideas of justice and individual freedom, as well as accepted concepts of resource scarcity.

The lack of consensus over the procedural and substantive norms of sustainable development presents a barrier to the implementation of sustainable development policy. Some writers have described an "environmental policy paradox"; in this view, the substantive changes that need to be made are clear. The paradox is that despite widely held consensus over needed policy changes, implementation is both slow and difficult (Smith 1992). In our work, we found not only a lack of consensus over goals, but a resistance among policy makers to both planning and to environmentalism as well. In part, this was in response to economic concerns over a potential tradeoff between prosperity and environmental protection.

Other barriers to planning for sustainability can be seen as a product of uncertainty or a lack of information. Problems are complex, and the assessment of future consequences is uncertain. However, the lack of reliable information about the future is a permanent feature of the policy landscape. Information is used to make policy decisions which is found to be sufficiently reliable and well founded. Judgments about the sufficiency and quality of information in public discourse can be based upon the extent to which that information is in accord with prevalent political views and the character and reliability of its source, just as much as more technical judgments of methodological quality. Decisions are made, typically, using the information that is available and least contested. These incremental decisions about economic strategy, social policy and ecological health are made in existing policy contexts. The policies chosen in the existing policy contexts, whether based on explicit concern for some view of sustainability or not, together constitute a policy direction.

Input to the policy process that seeks to affect the sustainability of future policies must address existing policy conditions. In developing information for policy, attention must be paid to crafting the information to the policy audience. Typically, policy is made in focused policy contexts. While sustainability requires a holistic approach, current policy institutions tend to have limited institutional roles, short time horizons, a single area focus and a limited mandate. Policy makers, however, often bind their consideration of strategies to one specific policy area. For example, economic development strategies are chosen with regard to their likely economic effects. Not only is this approach to viewing the problem likely to produce unintended effects on the environment, in the medium to longer term, these environmental effects may constrain the success of the economic development strategy.

Another important source of resistance in the American cultural context is the idea that policy makers should not consciously work towards common goals. There is a long history of reluctance to allow extensive power to any one policy institution. In the history of institutional development in the United States, the mandate of single institutions has been limited. As well, the overall legitimacy of the role of government in development has been subject to question. Currently, policy institutions have limited mandates, and policy makers see their own concerns as legitimately limited to a particular policy area. There are institutional limitations on the extent to which policy makers are able to take a holistic view (Scheberle 1997). While there is not a necessary contradiction between limited institutional mandates and the pursuit of sustainable development, the substantive consideration of holistic effects is made more difficult both by institutional structure and cultural mores.

Nevertheless, all policy choices have some environmental impact. Some of the environmental effects of alternative economic strategies are significant and some might defeat the policy choice over the long term. It is important to consider environmental impacts, including those policy contexts that do not fall under the mandates usually understood as "environmental policy."

The purpose of the project we undertook in the state of Kentucky was to examine policy alternatives and identify policy directions that held the promise of sustainable development that would enhance both the socioeconomic well-being and the quality of the physical environment for the people of Kentucky. While the details of the policy context and the institutional context may be specific to that particular task, we feel that the approach we used is potentially transferable to other contexts. We designed a process directed towards engaging policy makers in discussions of sustainability and environmental consequences at the same time as it would ensure the relevance to policy makers of the forecasts we produced.

The methodological contributions presented in this book include a unique mix of forecasting techniques, which include techniques that tailor the forecast to its intended policy audience and its social and political context. Methodological attention in forecasting often places more emphasis on rigor than on policy relevance. Our approach emphasizes that forecasts must speak to policy makers' current opinions. The methodological innovations we describe include techniques for ensuring that policy input is found to be feasible, relevant, focused and viable by a given policy audience.

We describe a unique application of nominal group technique and utilization of the cross-impact matrix technique to the process of deriving planning foci and alternative paths. The group methods and their utilization are central to producing a planning product that is focused on the issues currently considered salient by opinion and policy leaders in a nation or state.

3

This focus does translate directly into our substantive results. For example, we used the assessments of current policy actors to frame the assumptions about what degree of cultural, attitudinal and behavioral changes were believable or achievable. This rather limited possibility was incorporated into the scenarios we evaluated. While we did engage in an active participatory process in deriving the possibilities on which to model scenarios and projections, this educational process, while valuable, resulted in incremental change in participants' attitudes. These changes could not be expected to affect all state policy makers.

Forecasting using the assumptions of the audience has this aspect of a mirror-like projection. This technique does not assess the actual possibility for changes in attitudes and behaviors, it incorporates a believable degree of attitudes and behaviors; this is desirable as a response to the current policy audience. Not surprisingly however, using the assumptions gained from our current policy audience, our projections showed that technological change offered more potential for ameliorating environmental degradation in the future than did possible changes in public attitude or behavior.

On the one hand, this might encourage current policy makers to devote more resources to technological changes than to public education. On the other hand, if the policy input did not respond to the assumptions of current policy makers, even this move towards societal sustainability might be unimplemented. Policy input can be usefully constrained; wider realms of socio-political discourse support ongoing cultural and political changes. Information intended to change current decisions must be framed to focus on issues currently considered salient by public opinion of policy leaders and decision-makers. There is therefore a balance that must be struck between the amount to which a given forecast can move toward more sustainable outcomes and the degree to which it must speak to current conditions. This balance can be justified by seeing the problem of moving towards more sustainable outcomes as a longer-term process involving many small steps. These steps include education, awareness, and gradual changes in problem framing.

In forecasting, we used a scenario, or strategic planning, approach in combination with econometric forecasts and cumulative environmental modeling. Econometric forecasts, which are the platform on which the economic forecasts discussed here are built, are well known. The environmental forecasting technique employed in our project builds on econometric forecasts to derive cumulative environmental impacts. The particular model we used is one of a number of alternative systems for accumulating environmental impacts. The mix of the two projection techniques has been employed for policy-making in less developed countries.

4

However, this is the first effort to use the mix of the two production techniques for planning and examining alternative development paths for an advanced industrial nation or part of one.

Through a detailed description of our experiences, gained in completing a study of economy-environment interactions, we develop more general observations on principles, process and procedures. Our objective is to take advantage of the lessons learned in the course of a project we undertook to forecast the environmental futures of various economic scenarios in the Commonwealth of Kentucky. Our experiences with this project provide the basis for a guide to the ways in which data on the environmental consequences of economic development alternatives — and even choices about how to minimize negative effects — can be generated without generating resistance to utilizing the information in decision-making. The project we undertook in Kentucky offers a good example of the procedural steps which policy analysts can undertake to move the policy agenda towards sustainability, both in helping to frame issues and in evaluating policy direction.

Projecting the shadow of humanity on the environment of the Earth

Human beings, like any species in an ecosystem, have an impact on their environment, whatever they do. The ever-larger technological capacity of humans enables us to have far more significant environmental impacts than most species. This capacity for harm, or for good, can be controlled and directed by human volition. The exercise of volition, however, presumes two key informational inputs. First, decision-makers must recognize the existence of choices, that is, alternatives for action. And second, decision-makers must understand, to some extent, the consequences of those choices.

The discipline of economics describes itself as the science of choice, and its analytical focus is on constrained optimizations. The focus of economic analysis is the logic and process of the allocation of scarce resources to maximize the value of some objective function. The field of planning complements economics in that it explicitly addresses the processes by which objectives are derived by a decision-making organism such as an individual, household, private firm, government agency, or society. Economic planning combines the two approaches and explicitly addresses the decision-making processes: both the objectives to be pursued and the actions to be taken to attain those ends.

The pursuit of economic development and efforts to raise the incomes and associated standards of living of some population is a generally accepted

5

public sector planning function. Historically, such public efforts have compared alternative development paths and strategies, strictly on the basis of narrow economic consequences, measurable in monetary terms. Some more elaborate planning efforts have incorporated considerations of the effects on social systems and other aspects of cultures and traditional values of different economic paths. Only recently have such planning efforts begun to recognize that efforts to improve the well being of a population — whether income or access to goods and services — may be undermined by their *environmental* consequences.

We begin, however, with the more fundamental issue, that of envisioning *any* alternatives — the idea that alternative futures can be contemplated and then attained through conscious effort. If an organism cannot conceive of alternative futures, or choices, then it cannot act to attain a preferred outcome and no amount of information about the future will be of any use.

Without consideration of the environmental consequences of economic development alternatives, decisions about the perceived options before a polity may be seriously flawed. Paths may be chosen that have long term — even short term — adverse impacts on human well being. A failure to consider environmental factors and predictable outcomes may skew either the formulation of objectives or the formulation of constraints on choices. These failures may be attributed to some combination of two key shortcomings of the decision-making processes. First, there may be inadequate data on the interactions between human economic activity and environmental conditions. Second, there may be decision-maker resistance to incorporating evidence about economic-environment interactions in the policy process.

Decision-maker resistance to the consideration of environmental impacts often occurs through the dissociation of economic considerations from environmental considerations in both institutional mandates and in customary approaches. The very process of generating adequate data to provide a basis for choices that are better informed about environmental consequences may generate decision-maker resistance to using the information. The impact of the data-generating process on the economic planning decision process must be considered in deriving and selecting means of projecting economy-environment interactions and ensuring that strategic economic choices are made in the context of strategic environmental considerations.

It is imperative that in order to promote both improved economic well being and preserve environmental quality, planners seek an appropriate balance of economic development and environmental protection policies. We must find ways to move towards a sustainable future, to allow people to accomplish their current economic goals without encumbering the resources and quality of life for future generations.

6

The why and how of forecasting alternative futures

As we have already noted, human economies and their immediate natural environments are inextricably linked. Attempts to demonstrate these linkages and to trace the connections between economic activity and environmental processes can take many forms. One may look at the efforts to shape economic development processes and directions pursued by planning bodies or political jurisdictions to determine public priorities. Alternatively, one may examine private decisions by individuals, households, or the business expansion efforts of corporations as the driving forces of economic change. The choice of focus may reflect ideology or political priorities, but the basic premise is the same when one considers the relationship between economic activity and the environment. Economic activities are also ecological and environmental activities with specific impacts on the quality of air, water, land, and other local natural assets.

The quality of the environment and local natural assets or resources can shape the economic choices of private parties or local jurisdictions. A despoiled environment can diminish the attractiveness of an area for development. Alternatively, a clean, healthy, aesthetically pleasing environment can actually serve as a stimulus to economic growth, whether through the in-migration of population or through new business development. Similarly, assets such as fertile soil, mineral resources, or particular land contours provide the basis for for-profit activities that could not be pursued in other settings. Historically, humankind has taken the topography of an area as a given in most settings. However, the Netherlands' centuries-old reclamation of land from the North Sea — and certainly the far-greater earth-moving capabilities developed in the latter half of the twentieth century — indicate that even land contours need to be considered as variables in decision-making with respect to economic activity and the environment.

Resource depletion poses similar choice questions. The sustainability of particular local economic activities depends on decisions made about rates of current exploitation of natural assets. The measurement of the sustainability of natural resource activities is usually approached using stock-and-flow accounting. This approach can yield tentative measurements of sustainability, dependent on assumptions about technology and what is known about costs of replenishment of the "stock." Additionally, measuring sustainability in this way depends on the assumption that the activity or the resource will continue to be valued in approximately the same way in future economies.

Economic and environmental conditions are increasingly intertwined as the new technologies for production and disposal employed by humankind can change the biological and physical environments in which humans live. The

7

environmental effects in turn affect human well being, but the tradeoffs between increasing incomes of individuals or of populations and the resulting environmental conditions are not well understood. On the one hand, it is clear that the unregulated pursuit of economic growth could jeopardize many environmental futures; this conclusion is clear from the history of resource depletion and environmental degradation. However, under some conditions, economic growth could improve local ecological conditions, particularly as household prosperity increases and empowers an immediate concern for health. The prediction of overall ecological outcomes of any one type of activity is difficult. As well, the ecosystemic connections of even current activities are not yet well understood; we do not know how to predict or account for cross-media pollutants or for discontinuous changes in ecological health.

The inevitable uncertainty is compounded as economy-environment interactions are assessed from a longer time perspective. Our project was set in the context of a time horizon of thirty years. This timeframe was set for us in the terms of our project. The degree of uncertainty grows, as longer time horizons increase the likelihood of a completely unpredictable event altering some baseline condition. The significance of environmental impacts and interactions shapes their importance for policy.

In order to plan for the future, we must first understand how economic policies and actions impact environmental health. Efforts to delineate or model the modern human impact on the environment have grown more sophisticated over the last few decades, since this was first attempted on a global scale. There are many differences between these efforts; the key differences are in purpose and in the approach taken to uncertainty. In terms of purpose, some modeling efforts emphasize the attempt to influence the environmental policy debate, while others emphasize the production of a more precise or accurate delineation of environmental impacts. The key differences in the approach to uncertainty are between complex systems modeling and scenario-based approaches. Complex systems modeling attempts to incorporate the uncertainty within a single model, using mathematical models of randomness, chaos and surprise. Scenario-based approaches are based on narrative futures; rather than delineating the precise outlines of any one future model, several possible futures are derived.

Modeling and strategic planning are tools that can be used to provide information to decisions that affect the future. Some of this information may change the way the current problem is perceived. While the future remains uncertain, modeling can clarify some of the most logical outcomes of current actions. In this way, modeling and strategic planning themselves can be considered to have effects on the future. For example, if a modeling effort

8

produces a prediction that changes current attitudes, it may affect current policy and current actions and therefore change future outcomes. On the one hand, the given model is no longer an "accurate" prediction of the future, but it may still be considered to be a successful model. Modeling for sustainable development is modeling which seeks to change current actions. There is a tension between the normative effort to produce the best possible projections from the best possible data, and the normative effort to affect current policy decisions.

The first major global environmental forecasting was undertaken by the Club of Rome as part of their effort to affect decision-making through raising awareness. The model that was developed did not account for behavioral or technological adaptations. As such, the predictions that were generated by this model were dire Malthusian outcomes of overpopulation and resource scarcity (Meadows 1972). The Club of Rome model and its predictions have been criticized; from the perspective of accurate forecasting, the key criticism is that adaptations do in fact take place. Current trends cannot simply be extrapolated to generate a prediction. However, simple extrapolation does illustrate the fact that current behaviors may be destructive or problematic. Forecasting of this kind is intended to affect current debates and current behaviors through the quantification — or logical enlargement over time — to illustrate the consequences of current behaviors rather than to predict actual outcomes. An extrapolative model can be used to raise public awareness about the need for change: to change potential outcomes.

One of the outcomes which followed the Club of Rome model is that over a quarter of a century of work on modeling human impacts on ecosystems or environmental problems has followed, with local as well as global models developed. Many global modeling efforts have been based on econometric modeling. These models are basically a complex and interrelated projection of current trends. Like the initial modeling done by the Club of Rome, these project the present into the future. Some of the more sophisticated models incorporate feedback into resource substitution, or account for technological change through feedstock rates. Still, this approach does not account for significant changes in values, behavior, and rates of resource use or presently unknown environmental impacts of current behaviors (Arinze 1994; Charpin 1986; Hughes 1999; Woodell 1989).

Efforts have been made to build models that take account of behavioral changes brought on through economic and distributive feedback in a more complex system. Some of these changes include value changes in the societies being modeled (Daly 1973; Daly and Cobb 1989; Flinn and Reimers 1974; Forrester 1971; Odum 1971; Stigliani *et al.* 1989). Global modeling efforts are currently being undertaken in a large project sponsored by the United Nations.[1]

More complex system modeling attempts to imagine and incorporate possible behavioral and attitudinal changes, technological changes and systemic changes in the global environment (Hughes 1999; Kay et al. 1999). Scenario-based forecasting is currently a dominant approach in the private sector and in many types of policy analysis. This approach focuses on managing uncertainty and unpredictability, as these are understood as inevitable features. Scenario-based forecasting involves creating a set of believable future narratives, and then testing alternative paths against them. Scenario-based forecasts test the elasticity of specific strategies. While the specific future is not predicted, a strategy that will be robust under a variety of futures offers greater security. Scenarios can incorporate nonlinear causality and change. A decision-maker can develop a combination of strategies that combine gambles, which bank on one probable outcome, with those thought to be safer under a set of possible futures (Becker and van Doorn 1987; Fost 1998; Perrotet 1986; Schwartz 1991). In practice, in order both to quantify predictable outcomes and identify problem areas, it is usually necessary to combine the two approaches.

There is a substantial conceptual and analytical foundation on which to base efforts to not merely measure consequences but to explicitly consider choices between alternatives for human action. Our work in Kentucky built on this foundation. However, in the context of our project, we found it necessary to respond to the current debate over the tradeoff between economic development and environmental sustainability.

Is there a tradeoff between economy and the environment?

There have been a number of recent efforts to establish the extent and characteristics of the supposed tradeoff between economic development and environmental sustainability. Many of these deny the existence of the presumed zero-sum problem, in which the total resources available for use or consumption are seen as finite. These studies have been complemented by an array of conceptual and theoretical efforts to make explicit the ecological impact choices that are imbedded in the selection of economic development paths. We review a number of these studies in this chapter to provide some background to the applied Kentucky case through which we can examine the political and other processes that shape the environmental impacts and economic development alternatives actually examined.

The anti-regulation rhetoric of the 1980s in the United States was driven by claims that there were massive costs associated with government constraints on economic freedoms (Goodstein 1994). More recent analysis supported by carefully gathered economic data has found that environmental regulations are not necessarily economically costly. Some of this research has been made possible simply by the passage of sufficient time to permit measurement of the impacts of regulations. Many economic arguments against regulation as a whole are not empirically defensible.

For example, in an examination of current income levels and rates of economic growth in the individual U.S. states there was a *positive* correlation between the strength of environmental regulations and overall economic conditions (Meyer 1992). Of course, the evidence of correlation would not be sufficient for those who believed that the stronger environmental regulations were a result of, rather than a contributor, to stronger economic conditions. However, a study supported by the Council of State Governments presented the case for environmental protection as an economic development tool. In this study, it was also found that environmental controls contributed to stronger economic performance (Marshall and Brown 1995). Similar findings were reported for the United States as a whole for both investment and employment, and for the states in the South with respect to employment in environmental protection businesses (Hall 1994; Goodstein 1994). A similar finding was made in a comparison of industrialized nations with respect to the systematic reduction of greenhouse gasses (Greer 1995).

In the 1980s, criticisms of the presumed high cost of environmental regulations did not take technological change into account. Concerns about the costs of regulation might well have been warranted in a technologically stagnant context. In the 1990s it became clear that the overall cost to the economy of the existence of emissions controls or of environmental regulations as a whole provided an incentive for technological change. The selection of regulatory control instruments may be central to the provision of such incentives (Common 1995; Organization for Economic Cooperation and Development 1995). Experience has shown that there is rapid technological adaptation to pollution control regulation. Even conservative economic commentators have since argued that the benefits of pollution control often outweigh the costs (Easterbrook 1997).

Decisions ought not to be made on the assumption that there is a necessary and simple tradeoff between regulation of human impacts on the environment and the extent of economic expansion in an area. The decision problem needs to be better specified, both with respect to the choices available and the objectives to be pursued. A first step toward such specification is the

11

identification and elaboration of the actual pattern of links between human economic activity and its environmental impacts.

Economic development paths and their ecological impacts

While all forecasts are inherently grounded in past experience, studies that compare alternative future paths differ from earlier work in environmental projection. Following the overall move in forecasting from econometric to scenario-based forecasting, the modeling of alternative paths allows for the incorporation of future uncertainty in policy analysis. This new orientation saw the proliferation in the 1990s of contributions to three distinct strands of research on emerging or future links between the economy and the environment.

First, efforts in a number of disciplines were undertaken to link expected economic activities to specific ecosystem impacts or environmental changes. Second, there has been growing sophistication in the fields of ecological and environmental economics, and especially in the development of new techniques for assigning economic value to ecosystems and environmental assets that are not exchanged in any monetized marketplace. And third, discussions of the available alternative economic paths have led to a flurry of new studies offering recommendations on preferred routes or policies that are superior to some alternatives according to some specified set of criteria.

To date, the reductionist and anthropocentric nature of policy debates concerning the linkages between economic development and environmental impacts has been taken by some as evidence that this proliferating attention is inadequate to address the real issues. Yet it must be recognized that any analytical effort intended to influence decision-making must first establish its legitimacy in terms of the criteria and objectives of those with the powers to choose. If an anthropocentric perspective is inadequate, then a broadened vision can be learned over time.

Experience suggests that a decision framework that is too narrow can and does change. The evidence exists in the experience of the past decades in environmental decision-making itself. Initial considerations focused strictly on financial impacts and immediately visible changes in Gross Domestic Product or other measures in the national accounts. These limited criteria are effectively obsolete today, as environmental and ecological considerations have come to be integrated either as elements of the objective function to be maximized or as constraints on the set of acceptable economic choices. Thirty years ago, these considerations were implicitly assigned a zero value. Today, they are valued from an anthropocentric perspective. In the decades to come, a more ecologically centered valuation may well come to be employed. The opportunity for such a perspective to influence human decisions is provided by the three new developments in approaches to the environmental consequences of economic planning choices: measurement of impacts, valuation of impacts and alternative paths, and the assessment of development paths in policy contexts.

Early assessment and measurement of the environmental impacts of alternative choices took the form of benefit cost analysis (Mishan 1967). The use of the benefit cost approach, including the assignment of monetary values to environmental assets, has continued into the present. Many approaches have been designed to develop dollar-value proxies for non-market goods, including willingness-to-pay, contingent valuation and substitution. Another approach to valuing environmental assets, and thus to measuring the environmental costs of alternative growth paths, emerged from the regulation process itself. In a study commissioned by the U.S. Environmental Protection Agency to report on the cost of environmental investments required by regulations, it was argued that a proxy measure of environmental value could be derived from the cost of protection (Carlin 1990). This effort, however, did not delve deeply into the job and wealth creation associated with the cleanup and prevention efforts.

Many studies have taken broader perspectives, generally derived from systems analysis, to the examination of different growth paths and their environmental impacts. Much of this work has addressed the measurement or prediction of impacts and has not been directly linked to the decision processes that resulted in the selected development patterns (Huggett 1993; King 1994; Stigliani, et al. 1989; Weisbuch, Gutowitz and Duchateau-Nguyen 1994).

Considerable research has been directed to improving the linkage between the decision process and environmental impact measurement. Several studies address this linkage through the development of environmental indicators and a system of environmental reporting. This work is related to a larger overall effort that bridges the analysis of economy-ecosystem linkages and that assigns economic value to environmental impacts, including environmental accounting and environmental performance measurement (King 1994; Maclaren 1996; Pearce and Warford 1993).

There is substantial variation among concepts of sustainable development and criteria for the measurement of sustainability. As such, alternative paths intended to represent sustainable development are subject to wide variation, and there is not an accepted objective function against which attainment can be measured (Aberley 1994; Bartelmus 1994; Hirschhorn and Oldenburg 1991; Lesh and Lowrie 1990; Pearce and Warford 1993; Redclift 1987).

13

Nonetheless, the conception of such economic futures presents the problem of comparison and choice between of the proposed sustainable alternatives. This comparison and choice problem forces the issue of how to value, or measure, alternative ecological states. Efforts have been made to perform this measurement in the commensurable terms that the optimization logic of economics can incorporate in decision-making. This measurement problem was actually joined well before the recent spate of writing on sustainability policy (Isard 1972; Hufschmidt *et al.* 1983; Krutilla 1972), and continues to be investigated (Büscher 1994; Jansson, *et al.*, eds. 1994). The difficulty in measuring sustainable development is akin to the difficulty in measuring the attainment of any goal, the value of which will vary between individual valuations of it as well as between states of attainment.

Opschoor and Vos (1989) were among the first to take the next logical step, that of identifying the economic tools available to shape development paths. They were premature, in the sense that detailed arguments in favor of one or another proposed or preferred route for economic development did not emerge broadly until the past decade.

Some authors have proposed general approaches to sustainable economic development strategy. The weaknesses of this approach, in our view, is the tenuous link between existing policies and those proposed. As well, particular economic strategies must respond to particular economic strategic situations (Duchin and Lange 1994). Other work does examine alternative paths from specific unsustainable present conditions to more sustainable futures for different sustainable societies (e.g., Pirages 1996).

The possibilities for movement towards sustainable societies have also been demonstrated through current examples of broad-based ecological planning (Aberley 1994; Selman 1992). In governmental practice, specific recommendations have been offered for national technology policies that could promote sustainability (Rejeski n.d.), and examples of the extent to which U.S. states are already pursuing more sustainable development paths have been illustrated (Scruggs 1995). At the level of national governments, the possibility of concerted actions to shape more sustainable and thus more stable economies has been broadly acknowledged. Within a market economy context, national government policies which would increase societal sustainability as a whole have been identified, in particular in the arenas of technology policy and in national environmental impact planning (NSTC 1994; Dutch Committee for Long-Term Environmental Policy 1994).

Overall, considerable work has been accomplished in the linkage of environmental impacts to economic activities. As well, progress has been made in the linkage of the modeling effort to the context of specific decisions and in the development of implementation tools within economic policy.

14

Problems in evaluation and measurement persist, but these problems involve the enduring issues of valuation and reduction in economics.

Our project: Forecasting Kentucky's environmental futures

The forecasting project we undertook was in the context of an existing policy process. Our initial goal was to respond to the opportunity to deliver policy-relevant input to an economic planning process concerning future environmental consequences. This gave us a set of constraints and opportunities within which we conducted the project. We needed to respond to a specific context, project, and specific project goals. We wanted our information about economy-environment linkages to be incorporated into the decision process; so, we needed to respond to a specific policy audience.

The Kentucky project was a response to the need to seek an appropriate mix of economic development and environmental protection. Kentucky has suffered deindustrialization and experienced extensive economic dislocations. Resource depletion, reduced demand and public concern had affected the major resource industries, and this decline was thought likely to continue.

In this context, Kentucky had turned to restructuring its economic bases in order to increase incomes and the quality of life of its citizens. A focus on the economy-environment interactions was felt to be necessary in this largely rural state in order that its people could pursue a satisfactory livelihood while, at the same time, preserving their environmental resources and heritage. A balance was deemed necessary to allow people to accomplish the goals they wanted to pursue today without encumbering the resources and quality of life of future generations of Kentuckians.

Our project was to deliver input that would evaluate the sustainability of various economic paths open to Kentucky as a whole. The alternative paths we were originally asked to evaluate were those that would be initially acceptable to Kentucky policy makers as a whole. While we wanted to change the terms of the economic policy discussion to include a wider array of environmental considerations, we also wanted our input to remain credible to our specific audience.

In light of this, we developed a tailored forecasting method. Building on the environment-economy forecasting literature, we developed a method wherein we could measure and incorporate the beliefs and attitudes of our audience in our modeling approach. We believe that for legitimate moves toward sustainability to be implemented, there is a need to respond to the current institutional context, and a need to demonstrate possible changes and possible futures to a potentially skeptical policy audience.

Uncertainty about the future is accompanied by uncertainty about sustainable development itself. The idea of sustainable development offers a vision of balance, not a clear program of action. There has been considerable debate about the various weights to be given to the elements that comprise sustainable development. Much of the discussion involves the definition of criteria that will constitute the condition of sustainability. This is valuable work; it is in this discussion where the eventual achievements of society will be measured. However, it might be that disagreement about the definition of sustainability would forestall agreement on a program to work towards sustainability. Determining where to begin pursuing sustainable development presents a challenge. What our project exemplifies is a process directed towards making choices more sustainable in the absence of initial agreement on all goals or conceptual definitions.

Note

1   The Global Environmental Outlook 2000 report will be available soon. Updates are online at [http://www/unep.org/unep/eia/geo2000].

2 Process overview and rationale

Our task in this project was to assess the relative sustainability of economic alternatives for the state of Kentucky. In large part, the project drew on available predictions of possible economic futures to structure our economic projections and scenarios. We focused the environmental assessment of economic possibilities on the issues of importance to current policy makers. Both the forecasting process we designed and the key issues we analyzed responded to the policy context and to the interests of policy makers.

The window of opportunity to provide policy relevant analysis of the sustainability of alternative economic policies was created in a specific policy context. The dimensions of this policy context helped us to define the project task with a focus on policy relevance inherent in the method. At the same time, the dimensions of this window of opportunity constrained the project in specific ways. Constraints on time, data availability, resources and project direction both limited the project and also helped to give it further definition. The political culture of state policy makers was both a constraint on the project and an opportunity to tailor our analysis of policy alternatives. The planning process was designed to deal with those constraints that limited the analysis and to respond to those that created the context of opportunity.

The policy juncture within which our project was conducted was a statewide economic strategic planning process, which intersected with another statewide environmental risk identification process. As these projects were ongoing, our team was asked to incorporate an environmental trend analysis into the larger economic strategy analysis. This created a potential policy audience for environmental forecasting at the state policy level.

Our task included the identification of the most sustainable and politically acceptable means of increasing economic well being. To be relevant, our forecast of environmental impacts had to respond to political constraints of acceptability and to beliefs about the issues of significance. Many state policy makers respond to a political context that is immediate and in which environmental sustainability is an issue relatively low on the horizon. As well, basic environmental services such as clean drinking water and adequate wastewater treatment are not yet assured statewide. We used two social research methods to ensure that this analysis was directed to the priorities of state policy makers: a nominal group technique for stakeholder issue identification, and a cross-impact matrix to identify areas of highest priority concern. Our analysis of longer-term policy options had to respond to the present context of concerns.

In response to the inherent uncertainty of forecasting, we defined our task as one of measuring the relative levels of pollution and emission rates under a number of possible scenarios and development strategies. This strategy minimized the inherent uncertainty and lack of precision due both to limited data and the unknown future. Given the best data available, the forecasts would yield results that were directionally reliable under various dimensions of uncertainty. We felt that this approach would yield information of direct relevance to selecting among alternative paths.

We were able to take advantage of an econometric model that had been created in the context of an ongoing state economic policy effort. This model responded to the regional concerns of state policy makers. As well, an environmental impact forecasting model was located which could be adapted to run with the state model, with some development. Given the time constraints of the project, there was no possibility to construct the ideal dataset. Using existing state data, on the other hand, increased the extent to which the data could be considered both objective and relevant. Most of the data had been gathered under state or federal mandates and had been produced in-house by the state according to state policy interests.

The next step was the construction of the basic scenarios of possible futures. The baseline scenario was constructed through extrapolation; the others were created using narrative techniques. Using the combination of data, models and scenarios, a set of structural economic changes was tested to measure the varying economic impact of different strategies. The most valuable result of the initial model runs was that the environmental conditions in the state would deteriorate under both initial strategies tested. This result highlighted both the seriousness of immediate environmental concerns, and the fact that under the policy and economic conditions currently considered possible, the economy is unsustainable. As an input to the policy discussion, this result is an important opportunity for learning. In further runs, we undertook sensitivity analyses of the potential efficacy of various environmental policy strategies under a set of possible scenarios.

The policy context: Opportunities and constraints

The forecasting project we undertook was directed to a specific policy context. The state government was attempting to set environmental action priorities through a comparative environmental risk assessment, at the same time as it was attempting to set strategic environmental policy through a long-term policy review. This policy context allowed us, in our role with the Kentucky Institute for the Environment and Sustainable Development (KIESD) at the University of Louisville, to assess the environmental impact of economic strategy for a specific policy audience.

There was both interest and awareness among policy makers about both areas of improvement in environmental quality and areas of priority concern in environmental issues. In the environmental policy arena, the state legislature had mandated an assessment of existing conditions in 1990. That assessment, by the Kentucky Environmental Quality Commission, had been completed in 1992 and its findings published (EQC 1992). Following that assessment, a comparative environmental risk project, called Kentucky Outlook 2000, had been launched by the state environmental agency in cooperation with the federal Environmental Protection Agency (USEPA). Through extensive public consultation and broadly representative technical commissions, the state comparative risk project undertook to identify issues of significant environmental concern and priority areas for policy action.

However, policy makers in the state tend to place economic strategy at a higher level of priority than environmental protection, and to perceive a potential tradeoff between economic development and environmental protection. Kentucky is one of the economically poorest of the states. Economic development, both rural and urban, has been a focus for Kentucky policy makers. Prosperity continued to be an issue as structural economic trends continued to destabilize traditional economic bases of the Kentucky economy. The restructuring of the 1980s in the manufacturing sector had been accompanied by continuing restructuring in the agricultural and primary sectors. An Economic Development Partnership Board had been established earlier in the 1990s with the mandate to plan for a sustainable economic future in the state (NREPC 1996). At the same time, established industries with entrenched political support, such as coal-mining and tobacco-growing, felt threatened by the environmentalist agenda and the concepts of sustainability espoused by environmentalists.

In 1992, The Long Term Policy Research Center (LTPRC) had been created by the state, as a legislative agency charged with research and analysis for state legislators. Legislators wanted the ability to better position economic policy in response to emerging trends, drawing on a broad, future-oriented context of analysis. The LTPRC was assigned the role of identifying emerging issues and future trends and providing state agencies and policy makers with analyses of the long-term implications of policies. To ensure that the future orientation was incorporated into state policies on an ongoing basis, other state agencies were required to respond to the reports of the LTPRC in their budgeting process (Childress *et al.* 1996). The LTPRC evaluates key economic policies for state legislators, agencies, and as an input to state strategic economic planning.

In its strategic planning role as a legislative agency, the LTPRC had been appointed to coordinate the future-oriented side of the state comparative environmental risk effort. This was intended to provide a parallel assessment of future environmental priorities to accompany the assessment of current priorities. The LTPRC contracted with the KIESD to assess the environmental impacts of economic strategies, based on forecasts of economic conditions and their interaction with state policies. As a legislative agency, the LTPRC was able to provide the forecasting project with valuable input concerning the interests and priorities of policy makers.

Drawing on ongoing economic and environmental research, our environmental impact forecasting project had the opportunity to provide environmental analysis of economic policy in this ongoing policy development framework. The concurrent state environmental risk assessment of existing conditions provided valuable data to our project, and helped in the identification of priority issues of current interest to policy makers.

To meet our goal of providing information that would have relevance for policy, we had to respond to the situational constraints. The policy context provided both the opportunities for input and constraints on the form and content of this input. We needed to meet the time and resource constraints of the policy-making window. We gained information about the policy audience both formally and informally, so that we could provide information that was usable in the current political context. Our goal was to move the policy dialogue in the direction of greater sustainability, while remaining responsive to current constraints.

Task definition: Opportunities and constraints

The Kentucky forecasting project was intended to inform the choice of an appropriate mix of strategies in the pursuit of economic development and promotion of environmental protection. Our central purpose was the systematic evaluation of policy alternatives against possible future scenarios. To do this, we measured the extent to which future economic scenarios affected certain indicators of environmental quality. We had been asked to advise a strategic economic policy process on environmental futures. In particular, we had been asked to identify environmental conditions that might at a future date become central concerns. In the context both of economic restructuring and current strategic forecasting practice we felt that a detailed environmental forecast would not be the most useful product.

While we chose to describe the process as beginning with task definition, this activity continued throughout the process. As well, the processes of checking the relevance and applicability of the assumptions and premises continued throughout the project stages. Data collection and model refinement also continued throughout most of the project time frame. The stages of the forecasting process were not sequential, but iterative. The design of the project process was also informed by experience throughout.

For this project, we defined sustainability as development that enhances both the socio-economic well being and the quality of the physical environment for the people of Kentucky. Initially, this task appeared extremely broad. This forecasting strategy would give policy makers the best available information to choose the most resilient economic policy strategies, measured in part by their environmental effects.

Overall, we felt that a scenario-based logic would be the most appropriate to the policy context. The evaluation of policies under a variety of possible futures is more valuable than the prediction of specific detailed outcomes. Scenario based forecasting directly addresses the uncertainties of the future. By creating scenarios, one can evaluate strategies according to their performance under various conditions. This enables the analysis of key issues (Perrottet 1996; Schwartz 1991).

In policy contexts, another reason for strategic forecasting is that decision-makers, regardless of their political views, can use comparative estimates in decision making without the suspicion that the forecast is ideologically driven. The logic of the scenario based forecast is that if a certain set of structural changes occur, then these are the outcomes we can expect, more or less. One does not have to rely on specific valuations of environmental risks or a specific view of a good outcome to find comparative information useful.

The policy context of the project also helped to define the understanding of environmental quality indicators. Indicators such as air quality and water quality are a) already measured by the state and b) were undergoing review in the parallel comparative risk process. The indicators were thus pre-defined as relevant to decision makers.

We did not frame the task as one of finding the best possible — or optimal — development strategy. We felt that a forecasting effort had to deal in a central way with the element of uncertainty, and we felt that uncertainty

21

should drive the forecasting design. For example, the question of optimization requires a degree of certainty over the values of many parameters which is not possible for a forecasting effort. Since the question of optimization was never explicitly addressed, it was not necessary for us to quantify the valuation of environmental impacts or lost economic opportunities. Instead, we defined the task as one of the comparison of specific possible alternatives. This allowed us to address the question of comparison under future conditions using strategic planning tools that are more appropriate for conditions of uncertainty.

The forecasting effort we defined was not intended to provide specific predictions of annual emission levels for different pollutants, important as such projections might be. While the quantitative tools employed permitted calculations of that type, a broad array of questions about the statistical reliability of economic forecasts and about details of the links between levels of economic activity and environmental consequences would exist for any forecasting effort.

At the same time, the forecasts of impacts had to be state-specific, relevant to current economic policy, reliable measures of different industries and different regional distributions. This requirement created a large demand for data. This demand is also relevant to the usefulness of the forecasts to policy makers. Information that is inadequately detailed or not specific to economic sectors does not inform policy choices between alternatives. As well, policy-relevant information must be defensible to a broad audience including those who might disagree with the conclusions.

The Kentucky forecasting project was expected to link the examination of alternative environmental futures to the state's comparative risk determination efforts. However, the "risk paradigm" excludes many of the issues that are considered to be essential elements of sustainable development (Manning and Rejeski 1994:1). For example, comparative risk tends to ignore time, which is critical to the issue of projecting more sustainable development options. Similarly, the risk paradigm describes current reality while the forecasting effort attempts to move toward definition of the preferred changes in that reality. In an even more pernicious effect, the risk paradigm's emphasis on humans as receptors of exposures undermines consideration of their role, and thus the role of a society or its institutions, as the creators of alternative future paths.

No examination of risks, however detailed, can be relied upon to lead to consideration of alternatives. In fact, the more detailed the attention given the nuances of the current risks, the fewer resources are likely to be available for examination of choices in response to those threats. It is characteristic of complex environmental problems that judgments must be made in the absence of complete evidence.

An example may be constructed from global warming arguments in the United States. Throughout 1996 and 1997, as the nation moved closer to defining its positions for an international conference on global warming, the opponents of action on global warming threats raised the volume of their objections to any current U.S. actions or constraints on greenhouse gasses. Their recurrent theme was the inadequacy of the definitions of the risk, the limited quantification of the changes to be expected, and the inability to specify the dates of irreversible climate trends or describe the precise effects of the warming process. In other words, those objecting to proposed decisions on possible actions that might be taken to reduce future risks (or increase sustainability) based their arguments on the inadequacy of current data on risk exposures. They used the absence of data to satisfy a standard of proof they had established to argue that no choice was needed or appropriate. Their position was clearly untenable for a number of small island nation-states that might well disappear in the next century at the current rate of sea level rise, although no one knows exactly when (Glantz 1991).

Another example of policy action in the face of incomplete information is provided by the Montreal Protocol on Chlorofluorocarbons. The Protocol was signed in the absence of complete and definitive evidence on the date at which the hole in the ozone layer would have become so large as to be irreversible. As well, specific and definitive data was unavailable concerning the extent to which loss of the ozone layer could render the earth uninhabitable for human-kind (Parson 1993; Benedick 1991). Inaction is an inappropriate response to an uncertain future risk.

Actions taken to protect or improve environmental quality make sense from the point of view of those engaged in protecting financial assets. One avoids risks that are not quantifiable at least as much as others, since the very uncertainty of the unmeasured or inadequately specified risks make them more dangerous. Some critics have pointed out that environmental policy is sometimes supported by large corporations who see the opportunities for profit in both a stable policy environment and in the provision of environmental protection services (McInnis 1992). Recent evidence of environmental risk behavior in real estate decisions attests to the extent to which uncertainty about the actual levels of risk lead to higher levels of risk avoidance (Urban Institute 1998; Yount and Meyer 1998; Meyer and Chilton 1998). The rational response to uncertain risks is to search for alternative paths of action and to select among them those that appear to pose the lowest relative risks.

To be useful, the project products had to be reliable to a broad policy audience. That is, the content of the forecasts had to be defensible to a wide variety of interests in the state. Uncertainty permeates the modeling effort, in the relative valuation of many parameters. The prediction of specific valuations can be politically charged. Any forecast must be understood as an estimate, or it is likely to alienate certain political and economic sectors. Forecasts that are too detailed are less believable — and less defensible on ideological grounds — than directional and relative forecasts. The evaluation of alternatives we undertook, although less precise, is more broadly defensible.

The approach we employed in the Kentucky project was the selection of the most appropriate means of approximating the environmental consequences of economic development alternatives. A relative risk approach provides usable information for decision-making in the present about potential risks in the future. This enables the commitment of current political, economic and social resources to some set of actions. These actions can be chosen consciously in light of current knowledge about their relative impacts on the risks to be avoided.

Identifying key areas of concern

The production of forecasts and scenarios that are useful to policy makers requires that the issue of political relevance be taken into account in every step of the process. In issue identification, in the identification of key areas of concern, and in the construction of believable scenarios, attention must be paid to the policy audience. Relevant environmental forecasts must respond to the constraints of political acceptability and beliefs about the issues of significance.

We were able to draw on various sources of expertise and experience in deriving issues of key concern for policy makers at state and federal levels. In our initial task definition process, we met with seasoned policy makers involved with both comparative risk and futures projects in the federal environmental policy bureaucracy. The U.S. Environmental Protection Agency (EPA) was providing funding for the comparative risk project, and we described our project plans and objectives and gathered feedback. As well, we used those meetings as an opportunity to gather contextual information and to scan data available from the EPA forecasting and planning teams for later use in modeling alternative policy and environmental factors.

In issue identification, we used two social research methods in combination to ensure that the analysis was directed to the priorities of state policy makers. An interactive process called a nominal group technique was used for stakeholder issue identification through brainstorming, discussion and an open voting process. Similar to the Delphi technique, nominal group techniques tend to produce more reliable results than individual surveys (Delbecq and van de Ven 1971; Jones and Hunter 1995; Singh 1990). A cross-impact matrix was used in the context of the nominal group technique to help identify areas of highest priority concern. This technique, developed in technology assessment, allows the creation of immediate feedback on the relative importance of a small set of issues (van den Ende *et al.* 1998). We used these sessions to gather input and guidance on key policy context changes and key current economic development policy areas.

Participants in this advisory process were selected both for their expertise as individuals and the breadth of interest each would bring to the group. Participant expertise was sought in both environmental problems and in policy issues of importance in the state context. As a whole, the group selected needed to be representative of a wide variety of state interests. Participants in these processes included state officials, environmentalists, business representatives, and personnel from the university sustainability center not directly involved in the project.

The advisory meetings proved to be integral to focussing the environmental assessment and forecasting efforts on conditions and possibilities in the state. Initially, they served to help identify changes in the policy contexts within which Kentucky needs to pursue environmentally sustainable economic development. The session participants then defined five economic sectors for detailed consideration and examination of policy alternatives.

The first step was to involve the advisory group in the identification of the most significant environmental issues facing state policy makers in the next 25 years. Initially, a long list of issues was brainstormed, and then narrowed to those with significant support in a priority setting exercise.

This initial exercise showed that the development of the ability to respond, react, adapt and correct environmental problems as they occur remains the characteristic priority of the advisory group. Accordingly, the priority placed on changing the *objectives* (i.e., specific aims or targets) of environmental policy — at least with respect to the environmental impacts considered to be important — was initially expressed as relatively low.

In developing the next step of the advisory process, we felt that an educational component had to address the risks of this incremental and reactive approach. These risks include acclimatization to lowered environmental quality, the possibility of unanticipated and irreversible ecosystemic damage, and the key assumption that current knowledge of environmental conditions is adequate.

25

The next step in the nominal group process involved further priority setting exercises, along with a review and learning process. Contextual information developed by the project team was presented. As well, the project team presented the group with an analysis of the assumptions and accompanying risks of the issues and priorities identified in the first session.

In another voting process, participants narrowed the key environmental issues to five through priority voting. The five issues chosen were seen as most likely to affect actual environmental outcomes in the state, whatever the future economic development, due to their impacts on other policies. The most important policy issue selected by the group was environmental literacy in the state as a whole. As well, sustainable development policy, the need for leadership, critical public works and changes in energy usage were identified as critical issues in environmental policy.

Later, these issue areas were clarified by the project team and resubmitted to the advisory group for discussion and feedback in envoing sessions. The issue areas identified make up the arenas of change that the participants thought would shape the pressures for and boundaries on change in environmental policy and practices. In continuing work, it was essential that the implications of these policy issues be well understood.

The group identified five economic sectors in which public sector intervention would be most likely to have significant ecological impacts. These five sectors are the ones the group identified as most critical to current economic conditions and future environmental impacts. They arrived at the following list: energy (coal); manufacturing promotion and succession, production agriculture (tobacco), tourism, and value-added wood processing. Of the five, two are historically dominant industries regionally, and three are sectors that are seen as offering the most potential for future economic growth and development in the state. The consultative process, the use of nominal group technique and the cross-impact matrices, and our initial findings are described in more detail in Chapter Four.

The project team pursued this advisory input on the key policy context factors and economic activity sectors in order to focus its modeling and forecasting efforts. The objective was to expend resources only on the issues that a broader constituency considered important to the future of the Kentucky economy and environment. The policy contexts involved arenas for possible change in attitudes, tastes and regulations. These policy context changes could help shape the relationship between economic activity and environmental impacts in the state. These possible changes played a key role in guiding the construction of the different scenarios on environmental attitudes and technologies that were then considered in our forecasting simulations. The economic sectors, by contrast, provided the focus for the

26

construction of alternative economic projections. The baseline economic projection was constructed from projecting current trends in Kentucky; alternate economic paths were constructed from nonlinear changes brought about by more or less likely sectoral changes in economic conditions. The work of the project advisory planning group thus shaped the scenario analyses.

Data scanning

In order to meet the time constraints of the policy process, we also used data availability to limit the types of environmental impacts that could be modeled under different scenarios and strategies. Additionally, data quality was a limitation as data had to be regionally differentiated within the state to address state policy interests in regional outcomes. There is a high degree of regional differentiation in the state by types of industry, and both industry and activity specific impact data were required to calculate regional environmental impact projections. And finally, the project was required to respond to severe constraints in financial resources, which further limited our ability to pay for, construct, or recode the available data.

The best data were available for air quality. The quality and quantity of air pollution data available allowed it to be incorporated into the forecasting project at the level of analysis required for the project. These data were sufficiently disaggregated regionally, and our project could access them in a timely manner. As such, the environmental impact data presented in the subsequent chapters are primarily for air pollution. We were also able to make some limited observations on land taken for infrastructure, which can be associated with population levels and extent of urbanization.

The level of analytical detail in any project is subject to basic resource constraints. The two most common constraints in all research were present from the outset in planning for the Kentucky forecasting project. A final product was desired in less than ten months, so that it could be available for a legislative session. The report was supposed to be available at the same time as the results from the completion of the state comparative risk project, Kentucky Outlook 2000, as a future-oriented companion analysis.

Financial constraints were also severe. The federal environmental agency provided a base level of funding which limited the ability to construct custom models or data. We were limited to existing data and existing models, with some development. The base funding was also insufficient for more than casual personnel assistance. The state provided in-kind contributions. There were also limits on the ability of the university to provide data collection

27

personnel. The limited funds available for the project led the Long Term Policy Research Center and the University to turn to the state's environmental agency for the essential data collection functions.

The simultaneous conduct of the state comparative risk project did have a fortuitous effect on the quality of environmental risk information that was available and the level of its detail. This data was made available to the forecasting project team. Given the funding and other ties between the comparative risk and environmental futures projects, the state environmental agency assigned the comparative risk project personnel to assist in data gathering for the forecasting project. Nonetheless, when problems arose for the comparative risk efforts, the problems took precedence over our study, and ours suffered as a result.

The environmental impacts of alternative economic growth paths simply cannot be projected unless there are adequate data to link current activity to current releases and environmental conditions. For example, our project was able to locate eighty to ninety per cent of the data we needed to track the relationship between population, economic activities and releases of contaminants into waterways. However, using the existing software, we could not model projected water quality impacts without essential local water cycle data. The link between economic activity and water pollutant release could not be established and used in the projections.

Similarly, we did not have data on the amount and type of different kinds of fertilizers and herbicides used on acreage devoted to a range of farming activities. We could not say much about soil contamination impacts, nor could the contribution of farming to water contamination be traced. The data on farm chemical usage available from the state agriculture agency was reported only in terms of dollars expended per acre for the total of fertilizers, herbicides and pesticides. There was no differentiation either within the three classes of chemicals nor with respect to usage of the acreage in question. Even if the cost data could have been translated into tonnages, the failure of the data to link the chemicals to the specific uses of the acreage still prevented us from making use of it in our projections. The existing data collection protocol precluded the examination of farm product or land use alternatives in terms of their potential effects of the chemicals used, in type and in total, and therefore on the contamination levels of the runoff.

Despite our early efforts at determining the availability of data and assessing this availability against project objectives and key issues, data collection itself proved to be a critical limitation on the end product of the project. To a far greater extent than anticipated, our time on the project was committed to ongoing collection of data from state government offices and agencies. The data collection was necessary to inform the modeling of the economic, social and environmental conditions in the state. The regional assessment necessitated the incorporation of trend information on population, consumption patterns, travel patterns, energy sources and use, and current levels of emissions of pollutants. The full array of detailed data that would ideally be desirable for finely tuned forecasts of alternative environmental futures was not available. However, enough data could be gathered to provide indicative findings for major environmental concerns. More significantly, the logical process and the procedural and substantive importance of broad participation both in setting the parameters for the economic changes to be considered and the policy interventions to be contemplated can be discussed with reference to this project.

Whatever data on current economic activities and environmental conditions may be available, the information alone does not suffice. Some conceptual, analytical or computational systems must be accepted for (a) projecting expected or intended economic activities in the future, and (b) linking those activity levels to specific forms of pollutant releases, land utilization or other environmental impacts. Finally, the exercise of choice, and thus the decision process itself, must have a means of identifying acceptable current interventions that could shape future economic patterns, modify the environmental impacts of those activities or both. The Kentucky forecasting project used existing modeling programs to link econometric forecasts to environmental trends.

Project modeling elements

The modeling elements that allowed us to evaluate economy policy alternatives consisted of three basic elements. First, we adapted an existing econometric model and developed a set of possible and likely changes to develop a set of economic projections. Second, we modeled key economy-environment linkages for the state, linking an existing environmental impact assessment model to the state econometric model. Third, we assessed the environmental consequences of economic policies under these projections and then compared the likely environmental impact of possible environmental policy measures.

Despite the shortcomings of econometric projections in the long term, econometric modeling can produce useful inputs to forecasting in combination with other, more narrative approaches. Econometric and other time series models are widely recognized to produce poor results in long-range (multi-decade) predictions (Charpin 1986; Hendry 1995; Schwarz 1990). However, in longer term applications econometric models can be usefully combined

29

with a scenario approach, largely for sensitivity testing (Perrotet 1996; Schwartz 1998). In this context, econometric modeling can provide an analysis of likely and possible relative changes under different possible outcomes. The information that this forecasting technique provides to decision-makers is risk-based. The advisability of taking precautions against a particular risk that occurs with relative severity across several scenarios does not require faith in any one future possibility. While uncertainty about many of the outcomes of current actions will persist along with uncertainty about the future, certain kinds of risks are relatively predictable and actions can be taken now.

To ensure that an econometric model is useful for forecasting, a previously calibrated multi-equation model must be manipulable and must suit the context of the project. The ability to manipulate the model is vital to allow alterations in assumptions as well as to introduce the possibility of discontinuous change. Sensitivity testing of scenarios requires a level of detail sufficient to draw out useful implications from narrative scenarios. As well, the model must enable the analysis of changes in the policy environment and in potential public sector interventions which may alter economic development patterns. Parameters derived from past economic development patterns and paths should be replaceable by new constants reflecting intended policy or external economic pressure changes.

The basic constructs and statistical structure of any calibrated model sets some limits on the extent to which it can be manipulated and parameters can be substituted. Models are also calibrated for specific geographic areas and may not be appropriately applied to other economies. Some econometric models may be disaggregable into smaller geographic areas while others may not be. Thus the model employed must be subject to the manipulations necessary to reflect the policy or intervention choices contemplated as economic development alternatives are considered. A model appropriate to one decision-making setting may not be appropriate for another.

We used two different computer software packages to model the impacts of alternative policies. In our case, a regionally-specific econometric model and the personnel needed to manipulate it were available. The levels of disaggregation available in the model conformed to broad economic policy considerations in the state. We were able to specify a range of possible manipulations and alterations of existing economic trends. In order to develop a forecast of environmental trends from the econometric model, we were able to locate and adapt an existing environmental impact model as well.

To assess the environmental impact of different econometric projections, we utilized a model of economy-environment interactions that had been developed by the Stockholm Environmental Institute. The general characteristics of such emissions accumulation software are similar, so the particular model employed may not significantly affect the conduct or outcome of a similar projection effort. This software was selected on the basis of its availability and its compatibility with systems platforms available. The core of the model is a set of nested spreadsheets permitting the accumulation of different forms of pollutants from diverse sources. However, environmental impact modeling is data-hungry.

The environmental impact software was at an early stage of development. At the time, the software had been developed for contract, not in-house, users. The software had not previously been made available to any users other than its authors and their affiliates. Our project team had to engage in continuing development efforts with the software developers. This work included ongoing efforts both to assure the quality of the program and to develop efficient procedures for entering state-specific data for use in forecasting alternative economic and environmental futures. This experience is not likely to be replicated and does not warrant discussion here.

The particular tools we used are not the only resources available for conceptualizing the connections and the choices in other settings. Rather, like the other elements of our analytical process, the particular models we used showed both strengths and weaknesses in our forecasting effort. In Chapters Five and Six, we describe our modeling and scenario building efforts in detail, including descriptions of these strengths and weaknesses. The models we chose to combine in this effort were both suitable to the overall task and available within the constraints of the project.

Establishing the economy-environment links

Some aspects of links between economic activities and environmental outcomes are obvious, but others may be more difficult to track. Among the more difficult aspects of building such connections is the need to recognize cumulative effects arising across sectors and the ways in which shifts in the levels of different activities may either cancel out or enhance the impacts of changes in others. Automobile use provides one example of this problem; utilization of forest products offers another.

In order to reduce emissions from aggregate automobile use, one can either invest in urban public transport or in efforts to upgrade the emissions performance of automobiles on the road. In the former, the miles driven per capita may be reduced; in the latter, more efficient engines or engines in better condition may reduce the emissions per mile driven. If the funds for these activities were generated from taxation of tourism and increased tourism

31

were a major economic development priority, the emissions gains may be lost. In this scenario, automobile-based tourism could increase the effective number of miles driven in the state such that the net effect of the combination could be to increase the automobile emissions per annum.

The forest industry is a major source of economic activity in the state. Recent economic development efforts have been devoted to both increasing the volume of forest resources harvested and raising the level of value added forest production in the state. At the same time, new manufacturing processes have expanded the demand for what were previously considered waste products. The limbs and other harvesting waste were often left behind on forest floors when trees were cut for marketable lumber. What was "waste" is now an input into new processes and new products. Initially, turning waste into a manufacturing input might seem to be an opportunity for economic growth at zero net environmental cost. However, the former wastes were the fertilizer for new growth. As fewer "wastes" are left behind, the rate of forest regeneration might be reduced, dependent on soils. This environmental consequence needs to be considered in planning for the use of forest lands.

Any construct used to describe current economy-environment links and thus to forecast the effects of changes needs to be capable of tracking these sorts of interactions. In addition, it should have the capacity to automatically sum all the emissions of a particular compound from different sectors in order to describe the problem generated. For example, on objective might be to establish the net additions of carbon dioxide and other greenhouse gasses associated with a particular economic path in a geographic region. In this case, auto and industrial plant emissions of similar compounds might need to be combined. As well, the emissions-absorption capacity of forests or other ground cover may also need to be included. Using existing data sources in the computer models, we were able to model and compare the environmental consequences of different economic conditions for currently measured air quality indicators.

Identifying possible alternative development paths

The next element of our modeling process was the projection of possible economic conditions, both contextual and internal to the state, and the projection of possible economic and environmental policy scenarios. Our focus in this effort was also on issues currently considered to be critical by our policy audience and by a broader constituency. Our objective was to tailor our output to the needs and interests of our audience, at the same time. As such, we once again made use of input from our continuing work with the advisory group, the Long Term Policy Research Center, environmental scientists and environmental policy personnel from outside the state.

Our concerns in deriving the scenarios were that they should both provide a breadth of possibility to address future uncertainty, and that they should address key concerns of policy makers including their sense of what was plausible or likely. To gather input for the scenarios, we used formal and informal research techniques, document reviews and on-going consultations.

The project team pursued advisory input on the key policy context factors and economic activity sectors in order to focus its modeling and forecasting efforts. The objective was to expend resources only on the issues that a broader constituency considered important to the future of the Kentucky economy and environment.

The policy contexts involved arenas for possible change in attitudes, tastes and regulations. These policy context changes could help shape the relationship between economic activity and environmental impacts in the state. These possible changes played a key role in guiding the construction of the different scenarios on environmental attitudes and technologies that were then considered in our forecasting simulations. The economic sectors, by contrast, provided the focus for the construction of alternative economic projections. The baseline economic projection was constructed from projecting current trends in the state. Alternate economic paths were constructed from nonlinear changes brought about by more or less likely sectoral changes in economic conditions. Work with the project advisory group thus shaped the scenario analyses.

We continued work with the advisory group using nominal group techniques. Using the contextual changes and priority policy areas that had been identified in earlier meetings, in the latter part of this process, our focus was on the identification of key policy context changes and key economic development policy areas to test in our modeling. We used the latter meetings to explore the selected alternatives and to refine the nature of the changes addressed. The advisory group refined the issues to be considered in relation to the contextual variables. As well, they suggested criteria for selecting alternatives to current economic development practice in the five key economic sectors that had been identified.

We used a team-based organization to convene a series of meetings with both economic and environmental policy experts. We took advantage of the political acumen of the personnel of the Long Term Policy Research Center, the specific scientific expertise of faculty at the University of Louisville, and other sources of available expertise. These groups assisted in the identification of the relevant and viable policy choices for decision-making and their possible impacts on economy-environment interactions. As well, we

33

met with federal EPA personnel and reviewed EPA reports for use in modeling alternative policy and environmental factors.

Once we had our model assembled and some scenarios and projections for testing, we were able to assess the implications of current economic policy choices for certain environmental variables over time. Our scenario reasoning, preliminary results and further testing are detailed in Chapters Five and Six. Once we began testing, we found that within the constraints considered reasonable, no economic development path would be environmentally viable according to current standards. This finding is instructive and enlightening in itself. Without positing any conditions that were not believable or trusted, our model showed problems under any normal conditions. It was our hope that this finding would assist those who argued for environmental policies and education not currently considered feasible. Our response was to test our model for the policy combinations with the greatest impact across a set of economic projections.

The project process that we describe would probably not be replicable in other contexts for a number of reasons, some specific to timing, others to institutional factors. However, the process and the positive and negative impacts on the outcome of the efforts to identify the environmental outcomes of different economic development paths warrant review. While the sources of the project assets and liabilities in another context may be very different from those encountered in this state, the roles played by various contributing and detracting elements in this case may be instructive for efforts to conduct similar studies in other settings.

Although our assumptions were constrained in accordance with our audience's expectations and beliefs, we produced a report that recommended substantial changes in environmental performance over time. Our major finding was that action now is necessary in order to address basic health consequences under any economic policy scenario. This is an important learning, although not a palatable one. Beyond that, we were able to suggest the areas of greatest potential impact for state policy makers to address.

The report we produced through this process is set in the context of familiar industries; the industries of greatest concern in the state. The predictions are grounded in sources considered authoritative in the state and without leaps in cultural or political assumptions that, while possible, are unlikely to be believable to policy makers. Overall, we produced justifiable predictions about issues of concern to policy makers using their input. One of the innovative approaches we took in this effort was to tailor our report to the audience as much as possible. In the next chapter, we describe the initial stages of our project, in setting priorities and locating our project within a context.

34

3 Scanning context and setting priorities

Setting priorities has the effect of bounding the problem frame, of delineating what it is possible to consider within the scope of a project. This is a vital step in any futures project. It is dependent on the purpose of the assessment and on the potential policy audience (van den Ende *et al.* 1998). We had defined our task as one of comparing the environmental consequences of possible economic policy choices, as an input to the ongoing policy process. The existing economic and environmental context, including emergent trends, was also used to bound our analysis. This context would form the starting point of any path we chose to analyze.

For our project, setting clear priorities quickly was of the first importance, given our time constraints. We needed to respond to views of current conditions and likely paths that were widely held and accepted in the state. We wanted to provide input that would respond to policy makers current understandings, and move from there towards greater sustainability. Our initial task was to take stock of the existing context, information sources and perceptions, and to assess the need for project input by policy makers.

We used a two-stage model, beginning with a broad scan prior to gathering and assessing information in more detailed ways. This chapter describes the process of this broad scan and a brief overview of our findings. Our first step was to delineate the outlines of the socioeconomic and environmental context in terms of current conditions and future trends. The information and descriptions we used to interpret the project context came from official state sources for two reasons. Of most importance, we needed to set our project in an accepted informational context. As well, we had acceptable levels of access to these information sources given the setting of our project.

The second step of the broad scan was to evaluate perceived priorities, and to assess the difference between the priorities of state policy makers and those of state environmental experts. In this step, we designed and carried out a brief survey. We found that there was both interest and awareness among policy makers about areas of priority concern in environmental issues, although there were some differences between the perceptions of policy makers and those of environmental scientists in the state. However, policy makers in the state tend to place economic strategy at a higher level of priority than environmental protection, and to perceive a potential tradeoff between economic development and environmental protection. The economic and social context of the state is viewed as presenting a set of problems that are serious, that require action, and that are expected to present growing problems in the near future. Environmental conditions were seen as serious but manageable, and not likely to present new threats in the near future.

Kentucky — a brief socioeconomic sketch

The Commonwealth of Kentucky is one of the economically poorest of the states of the United States, and lags behind the majority of the states in many social and economic indicators. It is largely rural, with about half of its nearly four million people living outside of its small cities in agricultural areas and forested hills. Kentucky shares many economic, political and cultural ties with other southeastern states, while its urban manufacturing sector has more in common with states of the northeast and midwest. Population growth is moderate, and the population is regionally homogenous. Kentucky has a relatively stable rural culture that is resistant to change; the substantially rural nature of the state is expected to persist.

Long term economic restructuring has weakened three core sectors of the traditional Kentucky economy: manufacturing, mining and agriculture. In the manufacturing sector, the state underwent de-industrialization consistent with other rustbelt states in the 1980s and early 1990s. The resource industries suffered declines and adjustments throughout the 1980s; this has continued into the present. The coal industry was weakened through both resource depletion and reduced demand. Some reduced demand for coal is related to federal air quality legislation. As well, many farms in the state had been engaged in tobacco-growing. While tobacco farming had lost proportionately fewer jobs than other agricultural sectors throughout the last couple of decades, this industry is under increasing threat from litigation, legislation and lifestyle changes. The future of the tobacco industry is uncertain (Childress *et al.* 1996; Goetz and Schirmer 1996; LTPRC 1994; Smith-Mello *et al.* 1995).

36

Adjustment to structural changes in the Kentucky economy has been slow. The traditional economic drivers have not been replaced with equivalent activity in the new economic sectors. There has been some expansion in the service sector in the state, but it is small relative to this growth in the rest of the country. Small manufacturing firms have been enjoying brisk growth, but many of these are undercapitalized (Childress *et al.* 1996; LTPRC 1994; Smith-Mello *et al.* 1995). The state needed to restructure its economic bases in order to increase incomes and the quality of life of its citizens.

In the urban areas, unemployment is currently low. While the number of manufacturing jobs rebounded from the downsizing of the 1980s, manufacturing wages have been stagnant or declining. The skills of the labor force previously employed in manufacturing in the state are not those that are in demand in the new economy. The number of jobs in the newer sectors of the economy has grown at a slower rate in Kentucky than elsewhere. A large sector of the workforce has low educational attainment, and the transition from the old manufacturing economy to employment in the new economy is difficult. There is demand in the economy and in the labor market for the rising productivity that accompanies the information age economic shifts. (LTPRC 1994; Smith-Mello *et al.* 1995; Childress *et al.* 1999).

In the state as a whole, average household income and average educational attainment have been lower than national averages. As well, the growing gap between rich and poor has been wider than that in the nation as a whole. Poverty has been expanding as employment becomes less stable. The number of working poor households has been increasing. Family structures continue to change to higher proportions of single adult households with higher proportions of children living in poverty. Income inequality has been increasing (LTPRC 1994; Smith-Mello *et al.* 1995; Childress *et al.* 1999).

Among Kentucky regions, household incomes and educational attainment differ, with some regions well below state averages. The rural population is disproportionately involved in stagnant or declining economic sectors, such as coal and tobacco, which continue to show declining employment. Tobacco growing suffered less job loss in recent decades than other agricultural sectors in the nation, but many former tobacco growers are in the midst of restructuring, seeking new products and markets. The impact on employment levels is uncertain. The impact from declining coal and tobacco-related incomes is felt in the rural regions. The statewide trend toward an aging population is more pronounced in the rural areas, which is further exacerbated by youth outmigration. Outmigration is not as rapid as it might be in less tightly knit rural areas, but outmigrants tend to be the best-educated youth, further limiting the potential for rural participation in the new sectors in the economy (Goetz and Schirmer 1996; LTPRC 1994; Smith-Mello *et al.* 1995).

When we undertook this project, the economic and social trends which had been identified by the long term policy research agency of the state helped to set the context for our project. These are described more fully in Appendix One. Of the total of thirty-seven trends that had been identified, nine directly involved environmental conditions important in the state as a whole. For example, local government fiscal stress is on the increase due to rising levels of poverty. The capacity of local governments to respond to an increased demand for services is compromised by lower revenues. The environmental impact of local government fiscal difficulties is a limited ability to maintain or develop basic environmental infrastructure (LTPRC 1994).

The state of the environment in Kentucky

While socioeconomic trends indicate further weakening in some structures and continued low economic and social performance, public interest in environmental quality is high, consistent with those in the nation as a whole. There are significant problems in both rural and urban environmental quality. The state faces basic concerns with environmental infrastructure such as adequate wastewater systems, solid waste management and the provision of clean drinking water. As well, some anticipated changes in environmental regulations are expected to interact with economic conditions in Kentucky.

Kentucky has a land area of about 25 million acres. About half of this land is forested and hilly. The Appalachian mountain range runs across the eastern region of the state, which borders Virginia and West Virginia. There are significant areas of federally owned forest lands in the southern and eastern regions of the state. The north central region has gentler rolling hills and some grassland, supporting agriculture and horse-farming. The largest urban areas, still comparatively small, are in the north and west along the largest rivers. To the northwest, the Ohio River forms the border between the state and Ohio and Indiana. Tennessee borders Kentucky to the south.

In the early 1990s, Kentucky developed an assessment of the condition of its environment as part of an overall state bicentennial reporting effort (NREPC 1996). While air quality had improved since monitoring began with the introduction of federal regulations in the 1970s, the quality of drinking water has continued to be unacceptable. In 1995, more than half of the drinking water in the state was in violation of federal safety standards. While federal regulation has brought declines in toxic releases by industry, reported toxic spills have actually increased. Combined with toxic spills, inadequate wastewater treatment has led to worsening problems with overall water quality (Cole 1996; EQC 1992).

38

Groundwater contamination through inadequate wastewater infrastructure was of particular concern in the areas of karst rock formation, which is too permeable for conventional rural septic system treatment. The karst formations underlie a significant portion of the rural landscape. Inadequate wastewater treatment is a key issue in these areas, although toxic spills and illegal dumping also contribute to concerns about groundwater contamination. Some residents depend on this groundwater for their drinking water supply, although the proportion is not large (NREPC 1996).

The safety of drinking water in the state is related to local government fiscal stress. While the quality of drinking water in the state had improved over the prior decade, a significant level of state and local government investments is still required to bring all drinking water in the state into compliance with health standards. Along with inadequate wastewater treatment, increasing frequency of toxic spills had contributed to unacceptable drinking water quality. Further substantial investment in infrastructure is also required to treat wastewater and protect groundwater quality. New policies were needed to address both contamination and wastewater treatment. These were expected to focus on the source, rather than the cleanup, of water pollution. However, the ability to deal effectively with drinking water quality is limited by local government fiscal capacity (Cole 1996; LTPRC 1994).

Progress had been made in the management of solid waste in Kentucky. Over fifty nonperforming solid waste disposal sites had been closed, and those in operation were meeting health and safety standards. Participation in solid waste disposal programs was on the rise. In 1994, compliance was measured at eighty per cent. Legislation had been enacted that checked the flow of garbage into Kentucky from out-of-state, which had been destined primarily for substandard waste disposal sites (Cole 1996).

Recycling programs had been instituted, primarily in urban areas. Programs to promote waste reduction and recycling were expected to increase, as landfill disposal costs rose and more markets for recyclables become available. Currently, the state has waste and recycling legislation under consideration that would institute a refundable deposit on bottles and household waste pickup for every household in the state. These bills are controversial today and face a great deal of resistance. Local government fiscal capacity remains a constraint on waste management programs. Management of Kentucky's solid waste continues to challenge policy makers at every level (Cole 1996; LTPRC 1995; Childress et al. 1999).

Despite the high rating given to environmental quality in many public opinion polls, forests, lands and natural resources were found to lack protection and to be at risk from overdevelopment, overexploitation, pollution and toxicity (Cole 1996).

Health and safety regulations are having, and will continue to have, impacts on the tobacco industry, affecting the central agricultural region of the state. The federal Clean Air Act Amendments of 1990 are expected to lead to air quality improvements in urban areas when fully implemented and to have benefits to human health from reductions in harmful pollutants. At the same time, the new clean air regulations are expected to further reduce incomes in the eastern region of the state, currently the poorest region.

In this rural state, both economic and environmental conditions were regarded as important by policy makers and citizens. At least some actors in the policy development process felt that an assessment of the future economy-environment interaction was a necessary factor to consider in current policy choices. A more sustainable economic strategy was expected to enable the people of the state to pursue a satisfactory livelihood while preserving their environmental resources and heritage, and preserving the opportunities of future generations of Kentuckians.

The policy context

The policy context provided both an opportunity for input and constraints on the form and content of this input. Our project fit within an ongoing long-term strategic economic policy process, and in the context of an ongoing series of environmental assessments of both current conditions and action priorities. Within these larger institutional processes, the political beliefs and opinions of policy makers shaped their attention and concerns.

There was awareness and interest among some state policy makers about areas of improvement in environmental quality and areas of priority concern in environmental issues. However, economic development, both rural and urban, has been a focus for state policy makers. Many policy makers in the state tended to place economic strategy at a higher level of priority than environmental protection. As well, there seemed to be a perception of a tradeoff between economic development and environmental protection.

Kentucky's institutional pursuit of a joint objective of economic enhancement and environmental preservation was unusual for a state with income levels trailing those of the United States as a whole. However, the state has one unique institution that played a key role and provided the foundation for such a visionary approach to consideration of economic development strategies, the Long Term Policy Research Center.

An Economic Development Partnership Board had been established earlier in the 1990s with the mandate to plan for a sustainable economic future in the state (NREPC 1996). In 1992, the Long Term Policy Research Center

(LTPRC) had been created by the state, as a legislative agency charged with research and analysis for state legislators. Legislators wanted the ability to better position economic policy in response to emerging trends, drawing on a broad, future-oriented context of analysis. The LTPRC was assigned the role of identifying emerging issues and future trends and providing state agencies and policy makers with analyses of the long-term implications of policies. To ensure that the future orientation was incorporated into state policies on an ongoing basis, other state agencies were required to respond to the reports of the LTPRC in their budgeting process. The LTPRC was mandated to provide a biennial "trends report" on long term issues that require consideration in current decision-making. All agencies submitting budgets for state appropriations must justify their requests with reference to the trends to which they are responding (Childress *et al.* 1996). The LTPRC evaluates key economic policies for state legislators and agencies, and as an input to strategic economic planning.

In the environmental policy arena, the state legislature had mandated an assessment of existing conditions in 1990. That assessment, by the Kentucky Environmental Quality Commission, had been completed in 1992 and its findings published (EQC 1992). As well, state politicians and policy makers had been involved in the Rio de Janeiro Earth Summit. Afterwards, a conference involving state governments from across the United States had been held in Louisville, Kentucky. The conference was intended to bring sustainable development home from the Rio Earth Summit to all state governments. This national conference had the effect of raising awareness among many policy makers in Kentucky itself (Armstrong-Cummings, Barber and Stutsman 1994; NREPC 1996).

In addition to this growing sustainable development awareness within the state, the establishment of the LTPRC played a key role in the growing sustainable development policy agenda. With the establishment of an institution explicitly designed to force examination of longer term impacts of immediate political decisions and policies, Kentucky was bound to turn its attention to its environmental futures. The LTPRC was able to combine its work on new strategic economic policy with the sustainable development environmental policy agenda.

Kentucky was one of eight states to launch a comparative environmental risk project with assistance from the federal Environmental Protection Agency (EPA). The comparative risk assessments were directed to the relative valuation of environmental risks perceived and experienced by their populations. They were intended to be comprehensive and integrated risk assessments of current conditions within and across broad areas of environmental quality and risk. The comparative risk studies were intended

41

to help guide policies and programs at the state level and to provide political justification for potentially controversial public sector interventions to minimize some environmental risks. On the whole, the comparative risk assessment effort was more concerned with the allocation of limited environmental protection budgets across a set of response demands than it was with increasing commitments to environmental objectives.

In Kentucky, the comparative environmental risk assessment was called Kentucky Outlook 2000. It was launched by the state environmental agency in cooperation with the EPA. Kentucky's was the first attempt by any state to integrate long-term planning with the comparative risk assessment. The overall purpose, consistent with the other state efforts, was to allocate the financial resources of the state to the highest levels of hazard and risk. The Kentucky risk assessment was an attempt to derive bases for the comparison of risks, compare levels of risk from all sources and to prioritize policy attention based on the identification of highest priority ranking, in a broadly participatory and consultative process.

Kentucky Outlook 2000 was an ambitious project. The project relied on a Public Advisory Committee to define problem areas and concerns, with extensive public participation and hearings. The LTPRC was given the responsibility for a "Futures Track" within the overall comparative risk project. For the contemporary and comprehensive current risk assessment, three Technical Committees gathered data and provided findings on the severity of environmental risks in each of nine broad areas that had been defined by the Public Advisory Committee. Each of these nine areas was assessed for current environmental conditions and trends, risks and challenges, and possible policy responses (NREPC 1996).

The Kentucky Outlook 2000 process was intended to combine extensive public participation with the findings of expert panels on the measurable physical and biological hazards involved. The project relied on a nest of different committees, each with distinct duties so as to provide a broad mix of inputs and expertise to the problem. The Public Advisory Committee provided overall governance for the project. This committee was composed of various state and federal agency directors, the state governor and legislature, regional and state planning boards, environmental groups, business and industry groups, and other leaders. The Public Advisory Committee was charged with appointing members to the other project committees and subcommittees. The Public Advisory Committee served as the key problem definition body and as liaison between the project as a whole and the general public. Its broad membership was intended to provide direct project representation for all major interest groups in the Commonwealth. The committee developed the initial list of issues, oversaw public involvement activities, and reviewed reports produced by the Technical Committees. The final report from the project was intended to incorporate the response of the Public Advisory Committee to the Technical Report on relative risk levels (NREPC 1996).

At preliminary meetings in 1994, the Public Advisory Committee, with input from the Technical Committees, identified the nine general issue areas to be compared in the study: air quality, drinking water, groundwater, surface water, biodiversity, food safety, indoor environmental quality, land quality and waste. Issues of water quality had been divided into three areas in order to consider ecological and human health issues separately where appropriate (NREPC 1996).

Three Technical Committees were selected to provide expert insight into: (a) ecosystem threats and problems; (b) problems involving threats to human health; and (c) threats to quality of life. The latter category was expressly intended to incorporate factors other than environmental conditions posing threats to health and economic well-being. The Technical Committees were charged with directing the collection and analysis of data. Then they were to develop a ranking based on relative risk for these environmental issues. Each committee independently ranked the risk elements with respect to the factors for which it was responsible. Five steps were necessary in the full ranking process: hazard identification, exposure assessment, toxic effect determination, risk characterization, and risk ranking (NREPC 1996).

The Human Health Committee undertook to determine health risk to people from toxic agents associated with environmental pollutants. The Ecological Health Committee assessed the risk to the land, air, water, and biota. Both the Human Health Committee and the Ecological Health Committee were able to develop pathway effects models for each exposure analysis. The Quality of Life Committee considered the possible impacts of resource availability and land use changes on both the rural and urban human communities. In recognition of the multidimensional character of quality of life, this Committee derived eight independent ratings for the different issue areas, representing the dimensions of: aesthetics, economic effects, fairness and equity, peace of mind, sense of community, uniqueness, intrinsic worth, and recreation (NREPC 1996).

The different Technical Committees chose to use very different analytical approaches, that were appropriate to their particular area of analysis. As a whole, they decided to independently rank the degree of risk of the contributing factors associated with the three elements of risk. Each committee thus derived its own ratings of "high," "medium," "low," and "no risk/not able to rank" ranges of risk for each issue area. The committee as a whole made no attempt to aggregate these findings. Therefore, even though

43

the deliberations of the Committees were based in part on quantitative risk assessments, the findings in the draft Technical Report remained disaggregated, for an assessment by the Public Advisory Committee.

Unfortunately, we were unable to take advantage of the full potential of the information in this study, as it was conducted on a parallel basis to ours. The Outlook 2000 Final Report contained rankings of the relative priority of the different environmental hazards considered within each issue area. From this, a set of issue areas that should be given highest priority for state action could be developed. Difficulties in the systematic and integrated quantification of environmental risks are enduring. It is almost impossible to quantify some of the risks across areas in commensurable terms that are satisfactory and defensible to a wide cross-section of the population. Like other such efforts where this persistent disagreement is acknowledged, the study was unable to determine a final rating.

However, sets of priorities can be developed through this combination of technical and political effort. In each environmental quality area, areas of high priority risk were identified in each area of environmental quality: air, water, land, and waste. An assessment of future economic trends could use those current priority listings as starting points for future environmental analysis. It would have been an ideal framework within which to assess the tradeoffs between alternative economic structures and environmental policies we have examined in this project.

Because our project ran parallel to this one and was completed before it, our project was not able to incorporate the conclusions of this study. However, we were able to draw on this information as it developed. The priorities identified in the conclusions of the study were evident fairly early on in the process, and we were able to use some of this information as indicative of priorities as it developed.

Priority air quality issues included both local and regional pollutants. Mobile sources of both volatile organic compounds and ground level ozone received a priority rating. The primary source of this air pollution is from automobiles and other internal combustion engines. Although the immediate severity of health effects for the entire population was rated relatively low, the proportion of the population exposed was high, and exposure often exceeded federal health standards. Another of the highest priority risks was determined to be stationary sources of air toxics such as benzene, toluene and methanol. The severity of human health impacts was high across a range of possible health impacts, and there was determined to be a high level of exposure in localized areas. The population exposed to these risks was rated as high. Other significant air quality risks were found indoors, in tobacco smoke exposures.

As well, the study found chemical contamination of groundwater in limited areas to be a high priority issue in the affected areas, particularly in the region of porous karst rock. Sources of contamination were abandoned facilities, illegal dumps and inadequate wastewater treatment. Poor waste handling posed relatively serious problems for human health and quality of life, and affected land, groundwater and surface water quality. The assessment of land quality included such issues as soil erosion and contamination, biodiversity and food quality. Overall risks from these issues were found to exist at various levels of possible severity, but it was difficult to rank action priorities.

There is a diversity of political opinion evident in the reports of public input. Common concerns expressed included a distrust of environmental regulation and a concern over its potential effect on economic development and personal choice. As well, there were many participants who expressed concern over biodiversity, wildlife populations, the protection of surface and groundwater quality for ecosystem health, and the promulgation of effective environmental regulation.

The Kentucky Outlook 2000 project involved citizens from across the Commonwealth. It did contribute to the ability of the state to identify and prioritize environmental issues. Importantly, it also served as an educational experience for both the participating public and decision makers at all levels of government. Through an array of interactive processes and outreach efforts, environmentalists, industrialists, farmers, educators, and community leaders worked together to identify and consider environmental risks and their implications for the twenty-first century.

Our project was part of the Futures Track of the Kentucky Outlook 2000 process. The LTPRC had been appointed to coordinate the future-oriented side of the comparative environmental risk effort. This was intended to provide a parallel assessment of future environmental priorities to accompany the assessment of current priorities. The LTPRC contracted with us in our role with the Center for Environmental Management of the Kentucky Institute for Sustainable Development (KIESD) to assess the environmental impacts of economic strategies, based on forecasts of economic conditions and their interaction with state policies.

One reason for the LTPRC's decision to turn to the Center for Environmental Management of the KIESD was that the other research centers in the KIESD, as environmental scientists and experts, were heavily involved in the overall environmental risk project. The University of Louisville had just initiated the KIESD in 1993 and was anxious to demonstrate its utility to the state. The University was also willing to contribute additional funds to the futures project. At the state level, commitments to the provision of needed data on environmental conditions and resource uses were extensive.

Drawing on ongoing economic and environmental research, our environmental impact forecasting project had the opportunity to provide environmental analysis of economic policy in this ongoing policy development framework. The concurrent state environmental risk assessment of existing conditions provided valuable data to our project, and helped in the identification of priority issues of current interest to policy makers.

Within this policy context, the objective of our project was an examination of issues that might at a future date become central concerns. Due to the strategic nature of the economic planning process, we were not engaged in the conduct of a detailed environmental forecast or the assessment of the effects of changing economic or ecological conditions on forecasted conditions. Our project was explicitly directed to the evaluation of policy choices, consistent with its intended contribution to the work of the LTPRC. Our relationship to the larger Kentucky Outlook 2000 assessment was to use their work to inform ourselves of current conditions and the current issues of highest priority. We defined our task in this context as the examination of policy alternatives and the identification of directions for policy change that hold the promise of sustainable development and that enhance both the socioeconomic well-being and the quality of the physical environment of the people of Kentucky.

Setting priorities: The initial issue scanning survey

As part of our initial efforts to identify priorities and set boundaries on our work, we needed to evaluate the areas of highest concern to policy makers in the state: the intended audience for our forecasting efforts. Along with our scan of the context of conditions in the state, we designed and undertook a brief survey of policy makers and of those engaged in environmental research in the state. The purpose of the first survey was to gather preliminary opinion about the issues seen as having the highest priority for the foreseeable future. As well, we wanted to get a sense of any broad divergence in priorities that might exist between the policy group and those immediately involved in environmental science.

We chose to use a cross-impact matrix as our survey instrument. The cross-impact matrix design has been developed for boundary-setting and priority identification research, and has been most used in the practice of technology assessment (van den Ende 1998). The cross-impact matrix is intended to encourage respondents to think imaginatively about the interrelationships of trends and impacts.

The survey itself was designed to allow participants to identify environmental "hot spots" that warranted special attention. Our cross-impact matrix set environmental issues on one dimension and the change trends on the other. This provided a simple array of the key points on which this project should focus its efforts.

In accordance with the policy context of the project, we built on the work of the LTPRC and the comparative risk study. The output of both efforts was central to our first phase of forecasting problem definition. We drew from the issues that had already been identified in the two separate statewide planning processes. Thirty-seven patterns and trends affecting the state's future had been identified in a report produced by the LTPRC, and are listed in Appendix One. We used these as emerging issues in the context of change in our initial survey. We felt that the LTPRC list of emerging issues would help to locate our project in the context of a medium to longer term time horizon. Initially, we used the environmental impact areas as they had been developed in the statewide comparative risk project, and we regrouped these categories in the process of the survey.

The intersection of the trends identified by the LTPRC and the categories of environmental concerns defined by the Kentucky 2000 project may be said to define the environmental policy "hot spots" facing the Commonwealth. The intersections effectively map the array of economic and environmental policy issues that can be expected to confront decision-makers and citizens in Kentucky. Together, the two dimensions of the basic cross-impact matrix are comprehensive of emerging new policy issues facing efforts to promote economic development and environmental protection simultaneously. Both lists were constituted by an array of emerging issues and environmental areas that would have been already familiar to our policy participants. The initial assumption in using these two lists as a universe of problems is that no significant changes in policies, or in the outcomes of current approaches, would occur in the coming years. For the identification of initial priorities, this was a tenable assumption.

It was our intention to use the cross-impact matrix survey as a priority-setting exercise to evaluate the priorities of policy makers in the state. As well, we wanted to assess the difference between the priorities of policy makers in the state and those of environmental researchers. We designed our sample and our administration format accordingly. We selected two groups of respondents and administered the cross-impact matrix survey to each group separately.

Participants selected for the first group included academic faculty and staff from the research centers involved in environmental and sustainability research. These included specialists in environmental engineering and pollution prevention, environmental health, ecosystem sciences, environmental education, environmental law and neighborhood development, many of whom were participating on Technical Committees with the comparative risk assessment. We administered the first cross-impact matrix to this group of environmental researchers in an individual response format using a combination of mail- and hand- delivery. Our response rate was very high, since many of this first group were already involved in the comparative risk assessment and were aware of our work as related to theirs. In addition to asking them to identify the intersections of trends and issues of highest priority, we also asked them to suggest a recategorization of the trends.

The LTPRC trends had been grouped by topics that were not ideal for the assessment of environmental impact. We would have preferred a grouping by environmental impact potential or planning problem definition. As such, we also asked the research group to suggest an environmental impact-based re-categorization of the trends and patterns. We analyzed the results from the survey of the first group both for content and for similar patterns of intersection on the grid for different trends. Using this analysis and the suggestions we had received for issue regrouping, we regrouped the LTPRC trends. The resulting set of contextual trends was then grouped by change issue or causal factor in designing the survey instrument for the second, wider survey.

The redefined groupings were employed in a second cross-impact matrix survey administered to a broad group of state environmental and economic development officials, local officials, and representatives of the business community and environmental groups who participated as advisors to the project. The makeup of this second group is described more fully in the next chapter, as this group became an important part of our research process. Rather than an individually delivered survey, we used a focus group format. The survey was conducted during a first meeting of this group, following an introduction of our project as a whole. Since this group of respondents had an introduction and discussion prior to the survey, it could not be considered to sample a population of typical policy makers, or policy makers without exposure to environmental issues. However, our policy group sample had already been selected for breadth of representation on environmental policy, so it was already a non-random sample. We felt that our results could be considered sufficiently representative of the group of policy makers likely to be involved in the consideration of environmental policy. As a research design, the delivery of this second survey did not effectively sample policy makers without any additional exposure to environmental issues, but we were satisfied with the information we gathered from the results.

48

We were able to use the results from both groups to assess initial priorities for our project. As well, we compared the initial results from the survey of environmental science academics and researchers that we will call the Research Group, with those of the group of policy practitioners that we will call the Policy Group. Our results showed some key elements of common concern and some important differences between the two groups we surveyed. Although our ability to generalize is acutely limited by the small sample sizes in both panels, we could draw some preliminary conclusions and suggest explanations.

While important divergences existed, participants in economic and environmental policy processes and environmental scientists and educators were in considerable agreement as to the relevant and central trends and issues. As would be expected, the major hotspot area identified as critical by both groups encompassed the four trends grouped as environmental issues and policies: transportation, water pollution prevention, rising landfill costs and disease prevention. Their emphases varied, however. The Policy Group respondents overwhelmingly stressed air quality impacts, with waste issues a distant second. The Research Group, by contrast, emphasized land quality, followed by air quality, with the rest except for indoor air only marginally less important.

The consistently high ranking for air quality is understandable given the nature of sub-trends in this category; in particular that of transportation. The high concern for land quality on the part of the Research Group might be explained as a reflection of their predominant individual orientations. Many of those in the Research Group focus on land issues and many emphasize land use planning, physical infrastructure, and economic development.

The Research Group respondents actually flagged the set of new economic trends as the single most important set of forces shaping environmental futures, with land quality the major concern, followed by air quality and then the rest of the issues. The Policy respondent answers virtually ignored any possible environmental effects from the new economic trends that had been identified as emergent. For example, one of the trends listed was the emergence of secondary wood processing as a potential major economic sector. The Policy Group responses gave this trend minimal attention as having environmental impacts. Secondary wood processing had been given considerable prominence in policy circles as a sector showing the promise of significant expansion, in major reports from both the economic development and agriculture state agencies. We had expected that this sector would have been seen as important to the future of the state economy. As well, secondary wood processing involves the commitment of natural resources, and we had thought that some of its other potentials for environmental impacts might have been seen as important. The Policy Group did not seem to forge the connection between industry and environmental impact in their responses.

Additionally, the Policy Group respondents appeared to perceive no conflict between environmental protection and economic development. We had expected that this perception of conflict would be relatively strong. The Policy Group expressed a sustainable development vision. This result may actually be due to a perceived separation between economic activity and environmental protection. Or, it might reflect the fact that the Policy group members all had participated in an interactive and informative session before responding. Responses from the Research group were more likely to show a conflict between economic development and environmental protection. Responses from the research group had been collected individually prior to this first session and would have been more individual in nature. The Research group might not recognize the extent to which political compromises can be forged, which the Policy group knew full well.

After the group identified as environmental issues, the Policy group respondents identified education issues as the second most important set of trends. Ironically, the educators and academics in the Research group gave these issues relatively low weight as factors shaping environmental conditions. The Research group response might be representative of the "shoemaker's son goes barefoot" syndrome: as educators, they saw themselves as already addressing this problem. They might have been too close to the issues to see them.

The population pattern issues, while presumably linked to education, showed the opposite pattern in responses. Population patterns were rated the third most important group of trends overall in generating hotspots by the Research group respondents. The Policy Group gave population trends relatively little weight. It may be that the Policy Group viewed these trends as things over which they have little or no control. The scientists in the Research group, by contrast, might be inclined to list causes whether or not they are controllable. Also, the educators in the Research group were more likely to recognize the links between the population trends and educational trends. The Research group might even have interpreted the population trends as the causes of the education trends and therefore see them as both more fundamental and more critical.

The Policy Group respondents gave far more weight than did the Research Group to the issues that involved the balance between state and local governments that affect the policy environment and political capacity. The Policy Group identified the key environmental issues affected by this balance identified as, first, waste management and drinking water, followed in importance by biodiversity, with all other issues far less important. The emphasis on waste and biodiversity were echoed by the Research Group answers, with land quality as an additional issue and little weight given to drinking water. This difference seems fairly easily explained by the fact that members of the Policy Group are far more directly involved in the policy process than are most of the members of the Research Group. Most of the Research group respondents were not social scientists and had little experience with problems of program implementation.

The Research Group respondents did not see environmental impacts from the expected losses in traditional rural employment. These trends were rated the fourth most important by the Policy Group participants. The Policy group pointed to impacts on the environmental categories of biodiversity, land quality, and air quality, in order, as probable policy hotspots associated with rural employment declines. It may be that the natural science and engineering orientations of most of the Research Group respondents could explain this difference in perception of environmental effects from socioeconomic trends. As well, the Research group was primarily urban in location and orientation, while the Policy group had a more statewide perspective and was more attuned to rural issues.

Neither group of respondents considered that the trends involving impacts on children, crime trends, or labor market impacts would engender any potential sources of environmental policy or impact concerns.

Most people are not accustomed to recognizing the links between what are commonly perceived to be purely social trends and environmental issues. However, the failure to connect employment issues and environmental matters may mean than the responses overall reflect a common understatement of the potential for environment-economic development conflicts.

The task of identifying state policy hotspots on a grid seems relatively simple at first. The breadth and diversity of responses too is indicative of the need to systematically involve a range of different perspectives. Different groups have different ideas of priority areas for public sector intervention. These are related to their different approaches to problem definition. Accordingly, they also conceive alternative development paths differently. Clearly, the opinions reflect participants' backgrounds, occupational emphases and attitudes in addition to their specialized knowledge. Problem specification and solution creation done through a collaborative approach can take advantage of the breadth of various insights. Collaboration will result in a broader perspective and richer understandings of the development paths, intervention possibilities, and of mitigating or worsening environmental impacts incidental to ongoing economic activity.

Summary

At the conclusion of the first stage of the project, we had an initial list of priorities for our work. We had a working description of the current state of the economy and a sense of what the first priority environmental problems were in the state. Air quality was clearly a priority issue in environmental and policy circles. Drinking water quality, wastewater treatment and solid waste management were also important current and emerging priorities, with both significant environmental effects and important barriers to further improvement. We knew that prior to any intervention, that most policy makers did not immediately see economic issues as environmental nor environmental issues as economic. We also had an idea of what the difference in opinion and perception was between policy makers and environmental researchers as to priority issues for policy action on environmental issues. We continued to gather data from state sources as available and to evaluate approaches to environmental impact forecasting.

The constitution of an advisory group of policy makers was the next step in our project, and we had made a start on this task in the initial stage of information-gathering. We knew that we would need to keep an advisory group involved in further work to inform our project on an ongoing basis. As well, we wanted to involve this group in a social learning process. In the next chapter, we detail the process we used to gather more input on key issues using a further array of social research techniques, including nominal group techniques, focus groups and assessing feedback.

4 Social research for forecasting: Nominal group techniques in scenario building

We defined our task as one of measuring the relative levels of pollution and emission rates under a number of possible alternative development paths. The future is unpredictable. However, within a universe of possibilities that is infinite, there are some trajectories that are more likely, particularly given what we know of emergent trends and institutional inertia. A given strategy should perform well against a set of possible futures. The judgments of the likelihood, or probability, of the possible futures will affect the degree to which current choices take a given possible future into consideration. In order to affect current policy decisions, an effective forecast needs to engage current decision-makers not only in the identification of key variables, but in the construction and consideration of possible futures.

The future scenarios need to be constructed around a set of variables that are critical, or have significant impact, for a broad cross-section of economic, environmental and social factors for the people of the state. The identification of these critical variables is an important first step. The development of scenarios then becomes a process of creating narratives that produce significant change in these variables. Strategies, or alternative development paths, can be assessed for their performance against this range of possible futures. These performance assessments yield information relevant to selecting between current policies.

The scenarios developed need to be technically possible, economically feasible and considered possible by the policy audience. One of the difficulties in developing responsiveness to economy-environment

53

interactions is a limited conception of relevance in the current policy audience. Without any educational process, there is likely to be a much more limited set of variables that are thought to be interconnected and relevant across impacts and a much more limited set of futures that would be widely accepted as sufficiently probable. Both these judgments, of relevance and probability, affect the judgment of policy makers about sufficient importance or certainty to warrant current policy attention.

There is a tension between responding to the policy audience as it currently exists and ensuring that variables of future significance are accounted for in the policy process. On the one hand, our forecast had to respond to constraints on beliefs about issues of significance and the political acceptability of possibilities. On the other hand, our forecast had to identify and evaluate new and unfamiliar possibilities. We chose to address this combination of issues by using a scenario development process that involved a broad sample of those involved with policy making in the state in the consideration of possible or probable future impacts. This process included the introduction of new information and a consensus process of scenario development.

We applied a nominal group technique to addressing the problems of scenario building. This is a consensus building process with a high degree of responsiveness to issues of process which arise in an interactive setting such as levels of individual participation, and the prevention of group domination by individuals or coalitions. As well, nominal group technique has been found to produce high quality results and to result in a higher level of participant satisfaction than other consensus building processes. These considerations were important to us — we saw our research not as experimentation but as an intervention in the promotion of sustainable development.

The nominal group technique process involved the participation of a group representing a wide cross-section of state policy makers in a series of sessions. Each session addressed issues of immediate importance for our forecasting project. We used these sessions to gather input and guidance on the key policy context changes to test in the environmental impact model and key current economic development policy areas in which alternatives could be examined using the models.

We expected that participants in our scenario development process would frame problems differently as a result of their participation. First, they were exposed to a broader cross section of other policy stakeholders than they would have been in their normal day to day experience, and had gained understanding of the perspectives of others. Second, together they were engaged in assisting us in the creation and evaluation of futures. We chose to use this kind of consensus and information gathering process because it gave us more valuable inputs to our forecasts than a simple survey of current thinking. The drawback is that other policy makers, also part of the audience for our forecast, would not have had the benefit of this kind of educational and consultative process. However, we hoped that the quality of our results and the breadth of perspectives that they represented would help our forecast to communicate with this broader audience. We considered that our report would be responsive to their concerns but address them in a new way. We conceived of the report itself as an educational and informational intervention in an ongoing policy process.

The information we gained about key variables, significant economic sectors and environmental impact significance was used directly in our modeling process and in our scenario development. Our procedural findings in conducting this consultative process illustrate the singular importance of getting input and feedback from a wide array of sources. Initial opinions and judgments of relevance changed over time, as the participants were exposed to a wider set of perspectives.

Our findings highlight the evolutionary and developmental nature of thinking about environmental policy choices and the contexts in which they must be made. At the same time, we were aware that relevant environmental forecasts must respond to the constraints of political acceptability and beliefs about the issues of significance. In the context of our final forecasting product in this project, we felt that we were able to strike a balance between acceptability to a wider audience and challenge to current ways of thinking. The information we gathered through the scenario forecasting process, using the nominal group technique, played a key role in making our final product both acceptable and challenging.

Scenario forecasting

Scenario-based forecasting is currently a widely used approach to forecasting in the private sector and in many types of policy analysis. It is intended to allow a planning entity to prepare itself for many futures. The focus in scenario-based forecasting is on developing planning and response strategies, which are robust across a range of possible futures. Scenario-based forecasting often uses quantitative models for more detailed descriptions of possible futures and for sensitivity testing, in which the consequences of different strategies are tested against possible futures (Becker and van Doorn 1987; Fost 1998; LTPRC 1995; Perrotet 1986; Schwartz 1991).

Traditionally, modeling was intended to predict and describe likely futures. Basic econometric trend projection involves an extrapolation of current trends into the future. Given institutional inertia and the path dependence of the present, econometric modeling can produce relatively good forecasts in relatively stable times. However, this approach cannot account for basic structural economic changes, changes in behavior patterns due to new value structures, or other nonlinear change, whether adaptive or newly emergent.

Complex system modeling attempts to incorporate nonlinear change by modeling causal rather than patterned relationships. This allows the incorporation of feedback loops, and complex systems modeling offers the possibility of incorporating behavioral and attitudinal changes, technological changes, and to imagine and incorporate systemic changes in the global environment (Hughes 1999; Kay *et al.* 1999). While complex systems modeling often attempts to incorporate feedback loops and to model other sources of potentially large scale change, the future remains uncertain. When well done, complex system modeling offers better predictive accuracy than econometric modeling over a longer time frame. However, model building is expensive and time consuming.

Scenario based forecasting takes uncertainty and unpredictability as given. Given uncertainty and change, scenario forecasting provides an approach focused on managing with respect to the future. Scenario-based forecasting is a method of creating a set of believable future narratives, a set of futures, and then testing the performance of alternative paths of development. Scenario-based forecasts test the elasticity of specific strategies. While the specific future is not predicted, a strategy that will be robust under a variety of scenarios offers greater security. As well, the temptation to develop scenarios and use them as forecasts of a certain future has resulted in some misuse and misunderstanding of the scenario planning process (Becker and van Doorn 1987; Fost 1998; Perrotet 1986; Perry 1996; Schwartz 1991).

Scenarios can incorporate nonlinear causality and change. A decision-maker can develop a combination of strategies that combine gambles, which bank on one probable outcome, with those thought to be safer under a set of possible futures. Practically, in order to quantify predictable outcomes and to identity possible problem areas, it is usually necessary to combine the two approaches to forecasting and modeling (Becker and van Doorn 1987; Fost 1998; Mayer-Wittman 1989; Perrotet 1986; Schwartz 1991). In our project, we used existing models for scenario development and testing.

Within a universe of infinite possibilities, there are some trajectories that are more likely. The present, for example, is made up of a set of conditions, systems and trends. With benefit of hindsight, these conditions, systems and trends can be explained as changes in response to reasons through narrative history. That is, while we did not know in the past how the present would turn out, we can explain how the present came to be. Like the past, the present conditions, systems and trends have some inertia and are likely to continue, given institutional and social structures, unless sufficient change occurs. In the future, we will find ourselves explaining our trajectory, using narrative history, to make sense out of what happened in a story which starts in the present and gives reasons for the changes that occurred. The present is the starting point for a narrative about the future.

From a given perspective, like a state or other planning entity, there are certain changes that would have sufficient impact to change conditions, systems or trends of importance. Key variables are those in which changes will produce significant effects for a planning entity. The identification of key variables is usually easier for private sector planning. For example, multinational integrated oil companies would use the price of oil as a key variable. The price of oil rises and falls with supply and demand, technological changes, the security of global politics and the openness of trade. While the price cannot be predicted, the price is a key variable for the corporation (Schwartz 1991).

Key variables are often less clear-cut for public sector planning, but the concept of significant impact can be applied in the construction of scenarios for public sector planning as well (Ring 1988; Bryson and Roering 1988). For example, in our environmental scenario development for Kentucky, air quality indicators were a key variable. Many modeled activities would increase the level of air pollutants, absent potential technological changes or changes in the rate of pollutant generation. A rise in pollutant levels beyond a certain level of acceptability would have impacts on health, quality of life and on transportation.

The identification of key variables is an input to the construction of scenarios. In an iterative process of narrative construction and quantitative analysis, the range of values for key variables can be explored. Additional information for the scenario comes about through this narrative process. A possible value for a key variable is explained through a narrative development; this narrative development will have other implications. Using the example of air pollutant levels, improved economic performance without accompanying environmental controls or technologies would in many cases lead to a rise in air pollutant levels. A rise in pollutant levels beyond a certain maximum level of federal attainment would then have a dampening effect on the ability of the state to attract certain kinds of federal funding support, particularly for infrastructure improvements. This would, in turn, have a dampening affect on the capacity of the economy to expand given limitations on infrastructure.

Once key variables are identified, and a range of change developed for these variables within a narrative context, narratives can be developed which account for change in key variables within a limited number of change scenarios. There are a variety of key variable values for which a state should be prepared. The use of narrative for scenario development, rather than a set of values, is important to the effectiveness of the process. A narrative will explain the values of key variables, in such a way that the values are seen as possible and probable. This explanation prompts further thinking about the implications of such factors. A single narrative scenario can incorporate values for several key variables and allows an audience to understand the whole story. The narrative scenario can be developed such that its implications can often be modeled, using more traditional modeling approaches; a well-chosen set of scenarios can be modeled and the results will be informative. And finally, the narrative is easily communicated and is a more easily understood form of projection. This allows for wider participation in scenario development and a wider understanding of its implications. Narrative scenarios may even prompt faster response as narrative conditions may develop (Becker and van Doorn 1987; Fisher 1989; Kaplan 1993; Schwartz 1991).

In response to the inherent uncertainty of forecasting, we defined our task as one of measuring the relative levels of pollution and emission rates under a number of possible scenarios and development strategies. This strategy minimized the inherent uncertainty and lack of precision due both to limited data and the unknown future. Given the best data available, the forecasts would yield results that were directionally reliable under various dimensions of uncertainty. We felt that this approach would yield information of direct relevance to selecting among alternative paths.

For our purposes, scenario development was far more defensible than any attempt to generate specific forecasts. Our product had to be seen as defensible and reliable by a wide variety of interests in the state. Uncertainty permeates the modeling effort, in the relative valuation of many parameters. The prediction of specific valuations can be politically charged. In a policy context, forecasts that offer a range of scenarios are better understood as estimates and are less likely to alienate interest groups through perceived bias. Forecasts that are too detailed are less believable — and less defensible politically — than directional and relative forecasts. The evaluation of alternatives we undertook, under scenarios that were presented as probable, is more broadly and easily defensible.

In the private sector, the process of scenario development relies on broad-based analysis in combination with creativity. Consensus building techniques are used to develop scenarios, to increase line management buy-in and to improve managerial response to chosen planning scenarios (Ross, Schleifer and Switzer 1995; Mayer-Wittman 1989; Rowe and Wright 1999; Schwartz 1991). In scenario development, we employed an advisory board and involved them in a nominal group process. We used this approach to identify key issues of interest and likely impact, to prioritize these issues, and to develop a context of possible and probable medium term change. Our expectation was that participation would similarly increase buy-in by this group, as well as some of those who could see their interests reflected in the project report.

Narrowing the theoretically infinite range of options for economic development is more than a technical process. Whatever the range of options that are technologically and economically attainable, the politically plausible and sociologically and culturally acceptable alternatives will be a narrower subset. Along with the assessment of technical and economic possibility, the problem facing analysts interested in examining development options that are genuinely feasible involves a determination of the cultural and political boundaries on alternatives that determine their likelihood of attainment.

The nominal group technique

In order to develop scenarios and to focus issues, we needed to gather opinions and feedback from state policy makers about issues in state development. As well, we needed to assess judgments about the possibility of different narratives of both policy strategy and social and economic context. We knew that there would be a range of interests and opinions among our target audience; yet, we needed to narrow our issue focus and to narrow our range of scenarios down to a few manageable options. A standard interview could have measured the existing perceptions of a population of policy makers. However, we wanted to assess judgments about possibilities that were informed through discussion and exposure to the perspectives of others. Conceptually, this process is similar to an exposure to the views of others that might happen over time in a real world policy process. We reviewed participatory and consensus building techniques and chose to proceed using nominal group technique. This is a relatively open consensus building process that handles many process issues, engages participants in exploration and allows for the assessment of remaining disagreements.

Many interaction techniques may be used to elicit opinions, including focus groups, structured mediations over pre-specified issues and strategic planning exercises. These approaches may even lead to compromise and collaboration on specific elements or available alternatives. However, these participatory techniques are designed more as information gathering methods than as consensus building methods. As such, they do not necessarily engage participants in exploring and inventing alternatives, nor incorporate an educational or developmental process.

Overall, consensus methods are designed to reach a conclusion in the presence of disagreement and in the absence of conclusive evidence. The disagreement can be due either to lack of evidence, contradictory evidence or uncertainty. The best-known consensus methods are the consensus development conference, the Delphi process and the nominal group technique. Consensus methods have been widely used in attempts to measure the extent of agreement and disagreement, and to resolve disagreement and develop a consensus judgment. As well, they have been widely used in forecasting. Consensus methods must address group process issues such as domination of a group by individuals or vested interests, and the holding of untenable positions (Jones and Hunter 1995; Rowe and Wright 1999).

Performance assessments of consensus based methods have varied in their measurement of the extent to which good answers are likely to be produced. On the whole, consensus based methods have been found to outperform standard interacting groups, but careless application of the methods produces poor and invalid results. Care must be taken to ask the right selection of people appropriate kinds of questions (Jones and Hunter 1995; Rowe and Wright 1999).

The Delphi technique was developed three decades ago in forecasting and technology assessment. The technique is named after the Delphic oracle, which was to be consulted in times of uncertainty. The process involves the selection of a group of experts or qualified individuals and the individual interviewing of this group in a series of rounds. The individuals are asked specific questions and provide opinions or assessments, from their knowledge and experience. Typically, the opinions are grouped under a limited number of categories that show the ranges of disagreement. This information is given back to the individuals and their opinions are resurveyed in light of the information from others in the group. The process is intended to draw out consensus and dissensus through repeated sharing of group compromise or average conclusions with individual members. In most Delphi processes, the group never meets face to face. The product is an answer to the original questions posed that has an acceptable degree of consensus, and may include confidence or certainty rankings (Dalkey 1967; Jones and Hunter 1995).

The Delphi technique has been found to outperform both survey and standard interacting groups on quality of response. However, in addition to proper application of the Delphi process, both participant selection and task choice are critical to the success of a Delphi process and to the validity of its results. For example, asking the wrong kinds of questions or asking the right questions of the wrong group of people might produce a consensus opinion with no knowledge value. However, the Delphi process has been used well in many contexts. Because the experts are not required to meet, a Delphi process can involve a larger group and research can be undertaken at relatively low cost (Jones and Hunter 1995; Rowe and Wright 1999).

The Nominal Group Technique (NGT) was developed for in-house private sector management purposes more than twenty years ago. It uses some of the same concepts as the Delphi process, and is also designed to develop consensus opinions. Common elements include the involvement of experts, and procedural barriers to common group interaction problems such as group domination by individuals. One of the main advantages of NGT over Delphi is the structured method of measuring remaining disagreements and the strength of opposition to the group conclusions. While underutilized, the NGT process has much to recommend it. NGT is particularly appropriate for any effort that requires not merely temporary consensus formation, but also systematic insights into potential future conflicts and the likelihood that different alternatives may be attainable (Delbecq and van den Ven 1971; Fox 1989; Jones and Hunter 1995; Gustafson *et al.* 1973).

The NGT technique involves teams of 5-10 people working through a series of steps to arrive at relatively consensual responses to a question. In order to provide needed pressure for prompt decision-making and to discipline individual participants into conformance with group protocols, the NGT approach involves a minimum of three such teams working simultaneously in the same space. This arrangement fosters competition between the teams for creativity, which is essential at the starting point. As well, it also limits raised voices as participants don't want to attract the attention of teams at adjacent tables, while it permits some collaboration across teams as members eavesdrop on each others' deliberations. If the process involves a combination of teams for broader group discussion after completion of the initial NGT process, this prior informal interaction makes collaboration across all participants easier to attain.

The standard NGT process involves engaging each team in the following activities:

1 An initial briefing by team leaders and provision of the question to be addressed by the team. Team leaders are also team participants, although previously trained in NGT through participation in the process and then a briefing on the principles of the approach;

2 Silent generation of ideas and responses to this question by team members, writing on pads provided for the purpose (for 5-10 minutes);

3 Round-robin recording of ideas and responses on flip charts or another medium that all team members can see, soliciting one item at a time from each team member in rotation with no editing, in order to keep one person from dominating team considerations (15 minutes);

4 Discussion of the enumerated ideas and responses, so ideas presented can be clarified and individual items combined where appropriate (30 minutes);

5 Preliminary individual team member voting on item importance, anonymously rank ordering some prespecified number of items (5 is suggested) as priorities, with tabulation by the team leader (5-10 minutes);

6 Discussion of the preliminary votes, to clarify reasons for diverse opinions expressed and reconsider the combination of originally listed items, possibly modifying the item list (15 minutes); and,

7 Final individual team member voting on item importance, possibly for a different number of top priority items, with final tabulation and reporting by the team leaders.

Depending on the objective of the NGT exercise, the teams may then be brought together for discussion of the consensus and dissensus emerging across the teams. Possible subsequent votes on item selection or the redefinition of key list items are followed by a final vote (Delbecq and van den Ven 1971; Fox 1989; Gustafson *et al.* 1973).

Like the Delphi process, the quality of results which can be gained through an NGT process depend on the selection of participants and the validity of the approach for the questions and the issues addressed. Since there is a procedural requirement to select a specific appropriate group of experts, replicability is not an appropriate measure. However, there will be variability in the extent to which consensus is reached through consideration of the views of others and reasoned argument. Individual characteristics are likely to affect the degree of consensus that is attainable in ways that are not relevant to the question at hand. Some individuals are more likely to be swayed closer to the group consensus through peer pressure, some individuals are more likely to persist in unpopular positions. As compared to the Delphi method, the NGT technique has been found to increase performance by a small margin although it adds to the cost. Most importantly, the participants in NGT techniques have been found to be much more satisfied with the process and the results, probably due to the inclusion of face to face interaction (Jones and Hunter 1995; Roth, Schleifer and Switzer 1995).

Concerns with the validity of methods such as Delphi and NGT include the appropriateness of tasks and the appropriateness of participants. Participants in our NGT sessions and subsequent meetings included industry spokespersons concerned about the economic effects of stringent regulations, environmentalists worried about deteriorating conditions and a broad representation of government specialists from a range of different agencies. Other than academic participants employed as facilitators, most participants were recruited by the LTPRC in consultation with the state environment agency. This group included representation from regulators, regulated industries and environmental organizations, in addition to members of the LTPRC's own Board of Directors. This group was also constituted as an advisory group for our project.

The breadth of participation permitted the discussion to focus specifically on conditions, threats and opportunities in the state. The questions we asked were answerable in such a process. We selected a group of participants involved with the policy process in the state, using the advice of another policy office for expertise and appropriateness. From this group of participants, we sought judgments of issues that they were best qualified to judge, such as importance, perceptions of possibility, and likelihood of policy impact. Our construct of possibility was a practical, policy-related one that included technical, economic and political feasibility. This construct was consistent with our purpose in conducting the NGT. For our purposes, the issues or strategies considered impossible by a policy group are already excluded from the realm of policy issues. At the same time, we sought to expand the view of the group about what was possible or important and regarded the NGT discussion as an intervention as well as an information gathering process.

We utilized the NGT process for the first two of four planning sessions held with our advisory group to derive input on the key policy context factors and economic activity sectors, and to focus our modeling and forecasting efforts. Our objective was to expend resources only on the issues that a broader constituency considered important to the future of the Kentucky economy and environment. We gathered information on policy contexts, which we defined as arenas for possible change in attitudes, tastes and regulations that could help shape the relationship between economic activity and environmental impacts in the Commonwealth. The advisory group served to help identify changes in the policy contexts within which Kentucky needs to pursue environmentally sustainable economic development. Policy contexts played a key role in guiding the construction of the different scenarios on environmental attitudes and technologies considered in our forecasting simulations. Economic sectors, such as manufacturing or tourism, provided the focus for the construction of a projection of an alternative economy to that which would be constructed from simply projecting current trends in Kentucky. The session participants then defined five economic sectors for detailed consideration and examination of policy alternatives. The work of the project advisory group helped to develop the scenarios that were later modeled.

Meetings of the advisory group were integral to focussing the environmental assessment and forecasting efforts on conditions and possibilities in the state. The use of NGT assisted us in the identification of key issues, sectors and policy contexts. As well, the use of the NGT process in initial meetings assisted in the establishment of process norms. These norms were helpful in the interaction of the advisory group in subsequent meetings.

Identification of significant environmental issues

The planning sessions were essential for the derivation of politically and socially, not just economically or technologically, plausible and possible alternative futures for the Commonwealth. A total of four meetings were held with the full set of advisory group participants. Smaller meetings and telephone consultations were conducted later on specific Kentucky economic sectors. The first step was to involve the advisory group in the identification of the most significant environmental issues facing state policy makers in the next 25 years. Initially, a long list of issues was brainstormed, and then narrowed to those with significant support in a priority setting exercise.

The first meeting of the advisory group and nominal group technique session took place in May 1995. The success of the first meeting of our advisory group was essential to the successful launch of the advisory group process. A range of parties had been invited, spanning state government, environmentalist organizations and interested business representatives in the state. Nearly thirty individuals attended, representing a broad variety of interests. This group provided immediate guidance to the project, as well as an ongoing resource for future consultation. In addition, broad participation from Chairs of different Centers within the Kentucky Institute for the Environment and Sustainable Development assured the project access to expertise from across the Institute for construction of possible alternative scenarios for future policy environments, technological changes, and ecological and environmental impacts.

Upon arrival, participants were asked to split up into three groups, each to include a cross-section of interests. These groups were organized to permit the conduct of brainstorming sessions after brief introductory comments. They would also serve to permit examination of conflicts and differences in perception though the utilization of the Nominal Group Technique (NGT) for decision-making.

The session opened with a briefing on the project and explanation of the roles participants could play in the course of the identification of alternative futures. In order to stimulate thinking and consideration of issues, as well as to get people used to both participating actively and working with each other, the interactive NGT session was launched as soon as initial introductions were completed.

The project team followed standard techniques for the conduct of NGT sessions, with three teams of eight or nine people each selected from meeting participants. To maximize within-team diversity, each group included a cross-section of state personnel, industry representatives, environmental organization representatives, environmental officials, representatives of other public organizations and environmental researchers. The session opened with a briefing on the project and explanation of the roles participants could play in the course of the identification of alternative futures. In order to stimulate thinking and consideration of issues, as well as to get people used to both participating actively and working with each other, the interactive NGT session was launched as soon as initial introductions were completed.

Each team was assigned a facilitator, previously trained in NGT practices and principles. The facilitators, or team leaders, were the directors from the university environmental research centers. An initial briefing was followed by the introduction of the first question:

What are the most significant environmental issues facing Kentucky policy makers in the next 25 years?

The question was followed by a period for silent idea generation, and then the ideas were recorded on flip charts in round robin fashion, one idea from each member in turn. Following this process, group discussion and clarification of the suggested items led to some combination of the items with each other. The total number of items produced by the three groups for inclusion in their priority voting process was ninety-eight, about thirty items per team. The items differed widely in problem perception, scale, complexity and comparability. Several of the issues listed were ameliorative policy issues such as "recycling of paper, glass and plastic," and "hazardous waste disposal." Others were cultural trends such as "increasing, structural auto dependence" and "property rights issues." Others seemed to be aspects of the same problem, such as "lack of water quality data" and "protection of ecosystems."

Following this listing process, two votes were held, in which participants rank ordered a limited number of issues from the original list on the basis of projected importance. In the preliminary vote, the members of each group

65

were asked to anonymously rank order five items from the list their group had produced. Following this preliminary round, there was further discussion of the preliminary rank order, clarifying points of disagreement. As well, the groups made some further revisions of the items for voting. A second and final group vote was then held on item importance, this time choosing seven items instead of five. The larger number of items allowed was intended to measure the willingness of group members to compromise and to adopt outliers to satisfy other members of the team.

Seven items from each of the three groups (twenty-one items) were then presented to the group as a whole. This list had been distilled from the ninety-eight items that had originally been generated in the round-robin process. The entire group then discussed these items, with members of all three teams explaining their reasoning and clarifying their conclusions for each other. Obvious overlaps and commonalities were considered, as well as the loss of nuance associated with attempting to combine individual items into broader categories for voting and prioritizing.

The items in the list of issues were difficult to categorize. Taking the examples of property rights issues, one group named "property rights vs. Land use," in reference to the political context in which land use regulation was being challenged using the claim that land use planning constituted a broach of private property rights. Another group named "government as enemy," which could be grouped with private property rights in terms of political affiliation, but the "government as enemy" problem might be broadened to include a resistance to all environmental regulation or a resistance to expertise. The third group did not name an issue that could be easily grouped to these, as some common cultural resistance to regulation or to the legitimacy of regulation.

Our analysis of the ninety-eight ideas originally generated and the twenty-one priorities eventually identified at this planning session illustrated a problem in bias and response to proposals for actions or interventions that may prove problematic for decision-making to promote sustainable economic development. The difficulty became evident when we analyzed the issues and classified them in terms of the root cause or underlying problem involved. Table 4.1 classifies the entries as to generic type of issue.

It is not surprising that the participants in this planning effort were most concerned over the intersection of social, economic and environmental issues. The need to improve economic well being is clearly an important issue in the Commonwealth, and concern over the effects of environmental policies on the potential to raise incomes is understandable. However, it is noteworthy that only seven items listed out of the original ninety-eight specifically alluded to environment-economics conflicts. Given the total of forty-four issues identified under the general rubric of socio-economic policies and practices and the environment, it seems that issues of mores and values were recognized to be of critical importance in shaping future quality of life and environmental conditions in Kentucky.

Table 4.1
Initial listing of environmental issues facing Kentucky

Generic Topical Area	Team A	Team B	Team C	Total
Technical or Engineering	8	8	8	24
Lack of Knowledge/Data Problems	4	3	4	11
Policy Absence or Ineffectiveness	19	11	14	44
Social Problems/Environmental Issues	7	4	3	14
Socio-Economic Issues and the Environment	10	3	10	23
Economy — Environment Conflicts	2	4	1	7
Emerging Ecological Issues	9	5	4	18

On balance, the indication from these deliberations was that the highly publicized supposed "conflict between economic development and environmental protection" was not seen as a central "significant environmental issue facing Kentucky" by those participating in the first project planning meeting. In some instances, this type of finding may be attributable to the manner in which the issue was framed for discussion. If the discussions had been led away from perceptions of conflict, clearly this could not be defended as a strong result. In this case, however, the NGT discussion question, addressing "the most significant environmental issues facing Kentucky policy makers," cannot be said to lead either toward or away from articulation of a concern for environment-economic development conflicts. To a large extent, participants framed the issues themselves. The conclusion that no major conflict is anticipated may legitimately be attributed to the participant groups and not to the researchers or their procedures.

The unranked item lists did show limitations on the environmental perspective. First, there were a relatively low number of ecological issues listed as priorities. Ecological problems and species loss may only have been considered important insofar as those events have impacts on humankind that were currently recognized. Second, there were a large number of technological and knowledge-based issues identified; they outnumber the ecological issues almost two to one. This seemed to suggest continued reliance on technological "fixes." There seemed to be an expectation that advances in knowledge will always permit new problems to be resolved.

The project team then looked more carefully to see if the priority items gave a better understanding of the issues that policy makers considered to be critical. Table 4.2 displays the results of the priority voting across all three NGT teams for the four major categories exhibited in Table 4.1.

There was an extensive and problematic shift in emphasis between the different topic areas when the question was shifted from the existence of important issues to the identification of the most significant or important issues. First, we saw a major emphasis emerge on technological fixes. This suggested an objective function shift towards more, not less, tampering with the environment and complex ecosystems. Second, there was an acute drop in emphasis on knowledge and data problems. This drop was actually much more acute than Table 4.2 suggested. The single issue left as a priority by the participants was "environmental literacy" for the population at large, and none involving a concern for knowledge about the environment.

Table 4.2
Highest priority environmental issues facing Kentucky

Generic Topical Area	Original Percentage (N = 98)	Prioritized Percentage (N = 21)	Priority Items Total
Technical or Engineering	24.9	42.9	9
Lack of Knowledge/Data Problems	11.2	4.8	1
Policy Absence or Ineffectiveness	44.9	42.9	9
Emerging Ecological Issues	18.4	9.5	2

The results of the priority voting indicated that the focus group as a whole disregarded the possibility of critical missing knowledge, despite the participation of the academic researchers who may have stressed such issues. In effect, the findings from this first meeting suggest that state policy makers rely on critical assumptions and attitudes, the validity of which is increasingly questionable. Our analysis resulted in producing an explicit list of these assumptions. First, that adequate knowledge of environmental conditions — and measures of those conditions — was presumed to exist. Second, that the development of the ability to respond, react, adapt and correct will continue to be an adequate response. This assumption runs the risk of an acceptance of "short-term" environmental damage before adaptive measures are developed, if they are possible. And third, that the possibility of unanticipated and possibly irreversible ecosystemic damage that might adversely affect humanity is implicitly presumed to be zero.

These assumptions led to certain implicit priorities. Building an understanding of complex ecosystems was not a high priority. Further, the priority placed on changing objectives — at least with respect to environmental impacts — was relatively low. This current low priority was taken as a clear constraint on the alternative futures to be considered in project efforts to identify the changing policy contexts in which futures may evolve as well as alternative interventions in ongoing economic processes.

This initial exercise showed that the development of the ability to react to environmental problems as they occur remains the characteristic priority of the advisory group. Accordingly, the priority placed on changing the objectives, or the specific aims or targets of environmental policy was relatively low, at least with respect to the environmental impacts considered to be important.

Choosing impact priority from significant issues

The next step in the nominal group process involved a review and learning process, the identification of key arenas for policy action and a review of policy contexts. In developing the next step of the advisory process, we felt that an educational component had to address the risks of this incremental and reactive approach. These risks include acclimatization to lowered environmental quality, the possibility of unanticipated and irreversible ecosystemic damage, and the key assumption that current knowledge of environmental conditions is adequate.

In a second meeting, the advisory group first reviewed the efforts at the initial project planning session, revisiting the items initially recorded, the priorities identified and the assumptions evident in those priorities. The issues were next put into a context, with the group being provided with a broad synthesis of findings on internal and external trends to which the people of the state will have to respond, taken from forecasting and planning documents from the LTPRC and other Kentucky agencies and offices. The group worked to define and select, through priority voting, five issues from the original list of issues of significance for environmental outcomes across policy areas. A feedback process was undertaken to assure a common understanding of the nuances of the prioritized policy issues. These issues were: environmental literacy, sustainable development, leadership, public works and energy use changes. The most important policy issue selected by the group was environmental literacy in the state as a whole.

Following completion of this task, the participants then turned to proposed interventions into the state economy, using existing policy documents. The group then selected five economic sectors in which public sector intervention into the economy would be most likely to have significant ecological impacts. These five sectors were identified as most critical to current economic conditions and future environmental impacts.

The second collaborative planning session, held in June 1995, was not as well attended as the first, due to summer vacations and scheduling conflicts. Nonetheless, the group included representatives of business and environmental groups, the state environment agency and LTPRC personnel, other state government personnel and members of the KIESD. The participants first reviewed the efforts at the initial project planning session, revisiting the ninety-eight items initially recorded at the May session and the twenty-one priorities which had been identified.

The project team had completed an analysis of issue types from the issues identified at the first meeting. This analysis was presented to the group. This presentation and the discussion that followed was directed at the relationship between the types of issues on the full issue list and on the shift that had occurred in identifying priorities, using the data displayed in Tables 4.1 and 4.2. This discussion served two purposes. First, it gave participants a different perspective on what they had accomplished the first time they met. As well, it provided a review and background briefing for attendees who had been unable to attend the first session.

Next, the issues raised were put into a context of the trends of change in the state. Each team member was provided with information on internal and external trends to which the state would have to respond, and on some of the planned state-level interventions intended to shape economic futures. The first body of information given as background was the set of trends that the LTPRC had identified for strategic planning purposes listed in Appendix I.

Other information that was presented reflected expressed development priorities. We used photocopied material from economic intervention plans including a strategic plan for economic development which had been developed by the state economic development ministry, and an agricultural sector plan, also developed at the state level by the agriculture ministry.

Thirty minutes were spent in the nominal group teams, interacting with FKEF project staff and, discussing these trends and plans, and their combined potential significance for environmental policy choices and action priorities. The participants then operated as NGT teams to select five priority issues from the original group of ninety-eight items, taking the trends synthesis materials into consideration.

The NGT question employed in this iteration of the technique was:

Given the Trends distilled from Kentucky cabinet, agency and LTPRC planning and forecasting products, which of the 98 items recorded in the May issues identification meeting still belong on a list of priorities for this project?

This process, with discussion of the significance of different issues in light of emergent trends, initially identified nineteen issues as still salient and significant. Prioritization concluded with the isolation of five critical environmental policy issue areas in rank order: (1) Produce Environmental Literacy; (2) Sustainable Development; (3) Need for Leadership; (4) Public Works; and, (5) Energy Use Changes.

Based on the deliberations of the participants in both sessions, the project team then elaborated on the policy context changes to be considered as different possible scenarios in the simulation and forecast efforts of the project. The five policy issue areas identified framed the set of alternative policy contexts within which alternative tactics for attaining economic and social development objectives might be pursued. Definitions were developed for these issue areas.

"Produce Environmental Literacy" was intended to indicate the importance of an increase in people's understanding of the environmental consequences of their actions and decisions — and of the severity of the environmental damage done and risks now faced. The need to improve the understandings of adults was clearly expressed as a priority by the group; it is for this reason that they did not choose to call this issue area "environmental education." The group rejected "environmental education" as a term because it was understood as implying a focus on children and schools.

"Sustainable Development" was expressed to reflect two linked issues. The first issue was resource depletion and its consequences for economic activity, such as coal veins running out or too-rapid cropping of timber. The second was economic stability more generally, which is not necessarily an environmental issue except insofar as it generates uncertainty and fear. In this regard, issues were raised such as plant closings, loss of demand for tobacco and similar structural changes. Both reflect the social and economic interest in the ability to retain types of economic activity and associated communities of interest and lifestyles over time.

"Need for Leadership" expressed a common concern for public policy failures seen as associated with the reluctance of leaders to examine and pursue alternatives. The issue seemed to be that political and other "leaders" were not fulfilling their roles in the difficult exercise of decision-making in a political context. Given the other issues raised and those identified as priorities, this expressed need may be satisfied as the four other priority issues are addressed. That is, the apparent leadership "failure" may equally be due to an absence of real policy choices. Real policy choices could be derived from conscious study and articulation of options and an electorate that is aware of the possibilities associated with different choices.

The "Public Works" issue discussions indicated a high level of concern for the adequacy and quality of the infrastructure for transportation in Kentucky as well as worries over the adequacy of water and waste treatment facilities in the state. The transportation issues raised included mass transit as well as automobiles, and data transportation or electronic communications facilities were also mentioned. The issue thus is at least three-fold, covering infrastructures for transportation, provision of water for human consumption, and sewage treatment and disposal.

"Energy Use Changes" was a concern associated with the impact of changes in energy consumption patterns external to the state, not a concern with policies within the state. Subjects such as the sulfur content of coal, greenhouse gas generation, and alternative energy sources were raised in discussion of this issue. Given the importance of coal to the economy of parts of the state, this item was placed on the priority issues list. As well, it included questions of hydroelectric power generation potentials and possibilities of raising fuels for biomass in place of tobacco crops.

Following completion of this task, the participants turned to the evaluation of officially proposed public interventions, for their potential to move towards sustainable objectives. This task began with review of proposed interventions into the Kentucky economy, which were detailed in economic development and agriculture documents. The group was then asked to identify those categories of conscious public sector intervention into the economy that were most promising. The evaluation was to be based on those likely to be the most significant in ecological impacts and the most useful to consider in assessing alternative tactics for attaining the strategic economic and social development objectives articulated as concerns in the state.

72

The groups were then asked to enumerate five sectors for which alternatives should be considered. The group identified five economic sectors most critical in current economic conditions and ecological impacts and in which public sector intervention would be most likely to have significant impacts. The group arrived at the following list, presented in alphabetical, not hierarchical, order: energy (coal), manufacturing promotion and succession, production agriculture (tobacco), tourism, and value-added wood processing. Of the five, two are historically dominant industries regionally, and three are sectors that are seen as offering the most potential for future economic growth and development in the state.

These sectors then became the focus for consideration of the ways in which the state economy might be restructured. This discussion did not limit the method by which such restructuring might be achieved. Restructuring could take place either through the efforts of businesses and agencies in the state or under pressure from market, technological and regulatory forces operating in the national and global economies.

After this session, the project team reviewed the results of the two major portions of the process including the list of issue areas and the list of critical sectors. The team clarified the list of issue areas and resubmitted these definitions to the advisory group for discussion and feedback in later sessions. The issue areas identified make up the arenas of change that the participants thought would shape the pressures for and boundaries on change in environmental policy and practices. In continuing work, it was essential that the implications of these policy issues be well understood.

Developing scenarios: Social, economic and environmental narratives

The goal of continued work with the advisory group was to develop the material and input that had been named in prior meetings into modeling parameters and scenario narratives. The initial recorded results obtained through the formal nominal group technique sessions, such as the contextual changes and the priority policy areas, named priorities and provided a directional focus. Working with these, we engaged the advisory group in the exploration of alternatives to refine the nature of possible changes that we would address in our scenarios and modeling.

Project staff offered alternative interpretations of the types of contextual changes considered and of economic development approaches for the economic sectors that had been defined. The group refined the scope of the context issues, and discussed ranges of probability. The project team suggested criteria for selecting alternatives to current economic development

73

practice in the five economic sectors to be considered. At this point, we were involved in a parallel process of scenario development and testing through the use of econometric models, and the group was important to ongoing project issues and questions. Individuals in the advisory group were able to assist us in the modeling effort as well, with issues of data collection in particular.

Previously, no advisory input had been collected on the form of the policy context changes to be considered in the project, and such advice was needed. To facilitate discussion, participants in the third meeting were briefed prior to the meeting. We circulated an agenda, provided a list of the five critical context changes and our hypothesized implications for key model parameters. As well, we sent these participants information concerning the continuing project process, forecasting procedures, and areas for intervention alternatives to be considered.

At the third advisory group meeting, in July 1995, the project team first offered fuller definitions of the implications of the list of priority issues, to round out the five phrases we had as results. The participants agreed that our descriptions constituted reasonable summaries of the logic and concerns that had led to the phrases and their specified prioritization.

Next, the discussion turned to the key model parameters we had proposed and circulated. Participants discussed the preliminary conceptualizations of these changes for an hour and agreed to offer suggestions for modification, elaboration, and simplification of the list of contextual changes to project staff by phone, mail and fax.

We had introduced the purpose of our project as including a consideration of alternative tactics. Next, the participants in the meeting turned to the proposal and description of interventions. To the extent that planned approaches generated environmental risks or damages that might be avoided, the group discussed alternatives that might achieve the same ends. For each of the five economic sectors considered, the tactics currently proposed or in the process of being implemented constituted the status quo approach. The broad outlines of the status quo and a hypothetical set of divergent alternatives were presented to the attendees at this planning session in order to stimulate discussion about possible redirection that could alter environmental impacts while meeting criteria of political feasibility.

The hypothetical alternatives associated with a restructured economy induced extensive discussion of possible policy shifts, with some emphasis on changes that might take the form of shifts of emphasis or gradual adjustments over time. Participants at the meeting agreed to provide specific feedback to the project team and proposed a fourth meeting in addition to the three originally scheduled to identify the policy areas and alternatives to be simulated using the environmental impact forecasting model.

The fourth meeting of the full advisory group was devoted to two matters that were essential to fitting the project to state conditions and to the expected output from the comparative risk assessment process. The group first addressed data needs and related issues and then turned to an in-depth discussion of the specific economic sectors that had been identified as warranting examination for alternative futures.

With respect to our progress in modeling, we first reported on the problems of acquiring some of the data that we required to fully use the environmental impact model capacity. The data we were missing included activity, resource use, and emissions data. We requested assistance from the state ministry representatives present, and they promised their help and support. Other data sources, including nongovernmental resources were also discussed.

As well, no information on priority risks had yet been forthcoming from the comparative risk assessment. That process was supposed to have produced a listing of relative ranks assigned to different environmental impacts. As it happened, no information was likely to be available until the comparative risk process was due to offer an interim report in October, 1995, after our project would have been concluded. This was a matter of some concern. The group decided that despite this the our futures effort would continue. We would focus on building and refining the environmental impact model independent of any focus on specific environmental issues that might otherwise have come from the comparative risk project.

Next, the meeting returned to the five focal economic sectors: energy (coal); manufacturing promotion and succession; production agriculture (tobacco); tourism; and, value-added wood processing. We focused the discussion on what changes were possible in these sectors. Participants in the meeting were provided with further discussion briefs on the five sectors. The briefing sheet for each sector summarized existing economic promotion efforts in the area. This information had been extracted from existing policy documents as well as some critiques of those policies that had already been aired, and suggestions for possible alternative approaches. The objective of the discussion was to identify probable directions of change, if any, in order to guide our project team in generating a possible restructured economy. We wanted to evaluate the possibility that major economic shifts would improve or worsen the environmental futures of the state.

Participants voiced concerns over several developments considered to be possible. In the agricultural sector, participants expressed a concern over the impact of an 80 per cent decline in the number of tobacco growers and the effects of the associated income losses on families and communities. They saw a need to investigate the potential for new cash crops, including fiber, strand mill and biomass feedstocks from fast-growing woody plants.

In the manufacturing promotion and succession sector, participants saw a danger that current efforts might lead to deterioration in the air quality of the state. In most regions of the state air quality is currently high, and the concern was that "smokestack chasing" might establish the state as a pollution haven for some forms of air polluting manufacturing. Participants thought that an alternative that used a Community Development approach to business retention and expansion was important to evaluate, for its potential to increase local retention of the economic activity and gain. In this same vein, participants thought that linking manufacturing promotion to the resources available in the state was important, especially linkages to raw materials including timber and coal, as this strategy offered a similar retention and value-added benefit.

Participants considered that a good economic and environmental strategy would assure, to the extent possible, that the people of the state were able to maximize their economic gain from the available natural resources before they left the state. Again, the potential for the stimulation of new secondary wood products industries was raised as an example. On the one hand, secondary wood processing offers the promise of a vertically linked value added industry that offers greater economic benefits from a similar level of natural resource consumption. On the other hand, secondary wood processing industries can be quite polluting; pulp mills were used as an example. Environmental controls would be necessary to develop this industry in a positive way.

Participants were concerned about the impact of energy conservation efforts, and the potential impact of concern with global warming, on the demand for coal as a fuel. They also saw an opportunity for possible growth in the demand for coal as a petrochemical feedstock as petroleum supplies dwindle. The effects of oscillations in the demand for coal have economic effects that are currently geographically concentrated; some of these social impacts could be more widespread if coalmine shutdowns engendered more population mobility.

New forms of tourism were seen as promising. "Agro-tourism" is a growing sub-sector of tourism and involves visits to working farms and participation in their work. The state has many smaller and older farms that hold considerable appeal. As well, "eco-tourism" would take advantage of the Commonwealth's nature preserves and other protected ecosystems. Participants felt that it was important to assess the environmental dangers posed by a tourism strategy by expanded road use and worsening pollution from a proliferation of private cars on state roads. The scale of this problem would depend on the scale of tourism development, but if tourism became significant this possibility was felt to be worthy of exploration.

The group identified no specific policy changes for direct testing by our project team. The participants in the planning session recommended to project staff that in-depth analysis of different sectors, if conducted, should be pursued with private, university, and state government personnel who specialize in the fields. The advisory group also offered suggestions for people and organizations to contact regarding viable economic development alternatives to current sectoral development practice. In response, the project team had identified five teams of advisors to each address alternatives for a single sector. However, the information we had gathered through this process about perceptions of possibility was vital for the construction of our scenarios.

Summary of findings

Our project team pursued advisory input on the key policy context factors and economic activity sectors in order to focus our modeling and forecasting efforts. Our objective was to expend resources only on the issues that a broader constituency considered important to the future of the Kentucky economy and environment. Changes in policy contexts — attitudes, tastes, and regulations — could help shape the relationship between economic activity and environmental impacts in the state. These changes played a key role in guiding the construction of the different scenarios on environmental attitudes and technologies that were then considered in our forecasting simulations. The economic sectors, by contrast, provided the focus for the construction of alternative economic projections. The baseline economic projection was constructed from projecting current trends in Kentucky; alternate economic paths were constructed from nonlinear changes brought about by more or less likely sectoral changes in economic conditions.

The advisory group afforded guidance and parameters for establishing a project focus. The universe of economic policies that might potentially be examined is quite large. The advisory group made the research effort manageable by identifying what they viewed to be the most important policy contexts, issue areas, and economic sectors to be addressed. The work of the project advisory planning group thus shaped the scenario analyses.

The advisory group consistently named education, not just environmental education or literacy, as a major component of a sustainable future. Education issues were featured throughout the discussions. We observed that the consultative process engaged participants in communication and information sharing. The experience and changing perspectives of the advisory group illustrated the importance of education through this engagement. As the group was asked to think progressively more deeply about the issues, they adapted and refined their views. For example, their conception of economy-environment interaction changed from one in which there was little emphasis on economic trends to their perception as a central factor later in the process.

Our findings highlight the evolutionary and developmental nature of thinking about environmental policy choices and the contexts in which they must be made. There is a need for ongoing dialogue between policy makers, regulatory officials and those responding to regulatory controls, environmental scientists and engineers, and educators in the environmental arena. In our experience, while new information is constantly becoming available, the extent of misunderstanding and incomplete knowledge is great.

5 Environmental impact modeling from scenario projections

To compare the impacts of alternative development paths and public sector interventions, in combination with policy contexts and economic futures, we needed to be able to predict the impacts of different combinations of possibilities. To compare these alternatives and assess their impacts, we used two different computer models. An econometric model of the state economy was used for the basic economic analysis. It had been developed by the state and offered regionally disaggregated analyses. To develop cumulative environmental impact assessments, we employed an early version of impact forecasting software to predict impacts under these same sets of conditions. Through the comparison of the modeled scenarios, we were able to forecast relative differences between them in environmental performance.

The particular tools used in the Kentucky case are not the only resources available for conceptualizing the connections and the choices confronting planners. Similar models have been developed in a number of other forecasting projects. As well, the proprietary computer programs themselves have a growing number of available substitutes or competitors. Their characteristics, however, are indicative of the logical constructs needed to forecast and act on the environmental impacts of economic activities. Each element of the analytical process employed in our forecasting effort is described here in terms of its strengths and weaknesses. This descriptive and evaluative information should aid efforts to find comparable tools which to attack the forecasting problem in other settings.

Forecasting economic conditions and activities

Clearly, no effort to compare the environmental consequences in the future of current decisions on economic development approaches can proceed without some capacity to engage in economic forecasting. Such forecasts are the realm of econometrics, and some previously calibrated multi-equation model is needed for planning purposes. If explicit public sector interventions to alter current economic development patterns are to be evaluated in the alternatives to be projected, then the econometric model must be manipulable. The parameters derived from past economic development patterns and paths should be replaceable by new constants reflecting intended policy or external economic pressure changes. The forecasting model employed must be more than simply the output of some prior computer estimation: the model must be manipulable by knowledgeable operators who can force changes that simulate possible interventions.

The basic constructs and statistical structure of any calibrated model sets some limits on the extent to which it can be manipulated and parameters can be substituted. Models are also calibrated for specific geographic areas and may not be appropriately applied to other economies. Some econometric models may be disaggregable into smaller geographic areas while other may not be. Thus the model employed must be subject to the manipulations necessary to reflect the policy or intervention choices contemplated as economic development alternatives are considered. A model appropriate to one decision-making setting may not be appropriate for another.

Econometric and other time series models as widely recognized to be poor predictors for long-range (multi-decade) forecasts, such as may be inherent in any effort to predict cumulative impacts or to establish the environmental effects of current economic choices (Hendry 1995; Kay *et al.* 1999). These weaknesses, however, do not present a major problem so long as a comparative principle is employed in the choice logic. The decision framework is one of relative change or impact, not absolute levels.

The comparison rests on the assumption that the relative magnitude of even inaccurate forecasts can be an adequate basis for choice, in which case the errors in prediction would be similar in all alternatives considered. This assumption would be weakened if there were particular characteristics of either the econometric model or the assumptions about changes that are likely to induce biases in favor of one choice relative to others. The assumption would also be weaker if the driving forces or the systemic interrelationships of the economic system changed. Interrelationships might change in response to entirely new forces, values for variables outside of known ranges, or radical structural economic or political change (Kay *et al.* 1999). This possibility is difficult to address using existing models, although researchers can attempt to play out the implications of each scenario narrative. Once we began to review the results of our quantitative modeling, we felt that the implications were sufficiently strong for current policy. Given our purposes, we did not address the possibility of radical, systemic changes in this project.

Our economic forecasting process initially involved the development of our initial set of scenarios in quantitative terms. We used the information about priority sectors, emerging trends and policy context from our advisory group process, in combination with on-going consultations and document reviews. We chose a time frame of thirty years, to the year 2025. We sought a balance between an environmental time frame and an economic time frame; thirty years is a long-term economic forecast, but a relatively short-term environmental forecast. To generate mathematical forecasts of the combination of economic and environmental conditions, we combined the results from two existing computer programs.

We were able to take advantage of an existing econometric model and to utilize the expertise of experienced personnel who were available to manipulate the model and run our scenarios. The REMI econometric forecasting model had been developed for the state Legislative Research Commission by Regional Economic Models, Inc. It was available for our use, and it had a high level of acceptance by state policy makers as an "in-house" model. The REMI model represented the best available information on the state economy and its prospects. As well, the levels of disaggregation available conformed to broad regional policy considerations in the state. The model was used to provide basic forecasts of the state economy in the year 2025, and manipulated to project the economic and revenue impacts of alternative public policies and shifts in external markets and competitive position.

To generate predictions of environmental impacts related to the different economic scenarios, we employed an early version of an environmental impact forecasting model, called POLESTAR. This model had been designed as a decision support tool, to link environmental impacts to levels and types of economic activities. It had been developed by the Stockholm Environmental Institute and was used and made available in the US by the Tellus Institute of Boston. The POLESTAR program is an accounting tool that recognizes the environmental as well as economic inputs and outputs to an input-output interaction framework. POLESTAR links annual releases of pollutants to the air, water, and soils of a geographic area, rates of natural resource consumption and changes in land use patterns to levels of population and gross domestic product by major sector. Basically a complex set of nested spreadsheets, POLESTAR permits the user to introduce and then modify technical coefficients reflecting the unit levels of pollutants and other side effects of production and consumption. It links energy use to air pollution, for example, using information on the fuel used to generate the power consumed and the known level of pollution (particulates, carbon dioxide, and other gasses) associated with burning a unit of each type of fuel.

Once the current baseline economic model for the state was constructed, we used POLESTAR to test the effects of altering both policy context and economic context variables. One of the policy context variables we tested was the degree of environmentalism. This could be quantified as energy savings behavior and waste management behavior, as well as declines in the demand for state products such as burley tobacco or for relatively high-sulfur coal, automotive products and other manufactured goods. These demand declines would affect the economy of the state more directly. Policy variables we tested included alternative interventions in the economy such as the level and type of incentives offered and the modification of tax treatments.

We tailored the POLESTAR model to conditions in the state, to the extent that such technical information specific to the state could be provided. The POLESTAR model itself was disaggregable by region, economic subsector and process. This permitted us to perform regional analyses of the state, insofar as data were available. Similarly, POLESTAR could be used to address different forms of manufacturing production and shifts between sectors, changing agricultural product mixes, and variations in energy source mix, such as the use of different types of energy for motive power and electricity generation.

We generated forecasts for two different configurations of the state economy in 2025 and four distinct technological and policy change contexts. Through the advisory group meetings discussed in the previous chapter, we had identified the broad policy contexts to be considered and started to define alternative economic development patterns. Once the final set of contextual changes had been agreed upon and developed into scenarios of possible change, they were incorporated into the economic and environmental scenario forecasts.

The scenarios and contexts of change had to be translated into changes in parameters and variable values in order to generate quantitative alternative scenarios and contexts for comparison to continuation of current projected trends. We enlisted other faculty participants in the academic environmental research centers to help define the nature and extent of parameter changes to introduce into the baseline POLESTAR model. This activity was augmented by review of literatures on available and potential technological and cultural shifts and the likelihood of their adoption in advanced industrial market economies.

We relied on the Legislative Research Commission for the operation of the REMI model, and for the manipulations we required for our economic forecasts. The initial projection, of the current patterns in the Kentucky economy projected out for thirty years, was readily available. Our alternative "restructured economy" projection depended upon specification of the characteristics of a modified economy in 2025. When we provided that information, the Legislative Research Commission quickly generated the restructured projections. The population projections generated by the REMI model fit well with the independent forecasts generated by the Kentucky State Data Center at the University of Louisville and can be considered very reliable. The details of the gross state product projections reflect the uncertainty inherent in any long-term economic projections but are as good as those from any other source. The extent of the Legislative Research Commission experience in modifying the basic projections to test alternative interventions in the economy of the state and their impacts proved invaluable in interpreting the projections and in generating the projections for the hypothetically restructured economy.

POLESTAR is but one of a number of decision support systems that have the potential to enhance economic and environmental conditions simultaneously by contributing to sustainable development. We found POLESTAR to be extremely flexible and appropriate to our purposes. The extent to which it can contribute to improving decision-making regarding economic and environmental policies including taxation and subsidy efforts is dependent upon two factors. First is the quality and extent of the population and economic activity projections and the data available on current environmental conditions and the links between those conditions and different forms of economic activity. Second is the extent to which the policy context changes and alternative approaches to promoting economic development tested are realistic and well conceived.

Making the POLESTAR system operational for our project required far more time and effort than using the REMI model. The information required to run the POLESTAR model included the mix of current economic activity, the mean levels of emissions of different pollutants associated with production or consumption, and the levels of environmentally significant consumption. Environmentally significant consumption included such variables as per capita vehicle-miles generation, average miles per gallon for the existing vehicle fleet, household energy consumption, fuel and water usage by industry, and chemicals utilization in agriculture. We needed data on an array of pollution generating conditions and processes, such as: car and truck usage per capita (miles driven per year, by vehicle type); missions per mile (associated with fuel mileage, engine condition and the like); electricity, gas and other fuels consumed for lighting, heating, cooling and appliances or production (both by households and by firms distinguished by sector); emissions (air and water) associated with different production processes and industries; chemical feedstock used in production rates of agricultural runoffs (of pesticides and herbicides, and fertilizers, by type); waste generating and recycling rates, and net imports of solid waste for disposal, hazardous waste generating rates, disposal methods and associated emissions. The major limitation on our ability to take full advantage of the POLESTAR modeling capability were those imposed by the limited availability of data on the technical linkages between economic activity and environmental impacts.

The environmental impact data employed in this modeling effort come from agencies throughout the state government, as well as information from national and international sources. Data available specifically for the state was used wherever possible. One important factor in producing policy-relevant projections and scenarios is to tailor them to the extent possible to the geographic area to which they are to apply. We had to augment state data with those from other sources to find values for such items as emissions associated with different fuels, average fuel efficiencies for transportation, heating, and production. Our sources of data are listed in Appendix III.

For some variables, we used data that were available through the POLESTAR software itself. The program was delivered with the major data for a world sustainability model available. This model involved ten global regions, as compared to the four areas of the state model we constructed. Where we could not get state-specific data, we used the "North America" data from the construct developed by the Tellus Institute. The data for "North America" is actually a combination of data from the United States as a whole and Canada as a whole.

POLESTAR, however, is a data hog. It demands massive quantities of very detailed information, provided in very specific formats. Despite extensive efforts on the part of all concerned, state-specific information was not available for all the data elements we needed in order to generate the findings from POLESTAR that were of interest to us. The project team, the LTPRC staff and personnel from the state environment ministry involved in the comparative environmental risk assessment project, all attempted to gather this data and were unable to do so. Some data could be fully constructed for the state. Other data proved unavailable from either the POLESTAR world construct or state sources and could not be examined in the different scenarios.

Future research in projecting economy-environment interaction should become gradually easier as a result of related interest and research, as both data and impact linkages become established and as available modeling tools are improved. The version of POLESTAR currently available is much improved from the version we used, and is now downloadable from the world wide web. Like other software programs, it has undergone significant development in the last five years (SEI 1999).

As well, efforts to replace national accounting systems with full environmental cost accounting systems include data elements and economy-environment theoretical linkages that can be used to compare alternative economic development paths. National cost accounting research, while directed to the comparison of economic-environmental performance between nations, develops the relationship between economic activity and impacts on health and environmental damage (for example, World Bank 1996). As well, similar modeling and assessment is performed in the interest of cumulative impact assessment. Cumulative impact assessment research can also be used as a resource for the projection of economy-environment interactions (CEQ 1997). However, good environmental data remains difficult to find, and difficult to link to economic data due to differences in the units of collection and in different area and population impacts.

Our data problems had two implications. First, not all the environmental impacts of interest could be tracked and compared under the different economic projections and environmental policy and practice scenarios, most notably water quality. And second, the environmental impact results were less reliable predictions of the scenarios forecast than we would have preferred. The results could only be taken to be indicative. At the same time, we were still confident of the reliability of our results in terms of relative magnitudes and differences in scale.

The Kentucky regions analyzed — definitions and utility

The state of Kentucky is regionally differentiated. There are mountainous areas, wide-pen rural spaces and a number of cities of different sizes. To describe the economic impacts of policies or regulations, we needed to differentiate between different parts of the state. The REMI model used by the Legislative Research Commission distinguishes four regions, designated Bluegrass, Central, East and West. The Bluegrass region is bordered on the north by the Ohio River and is the most populous and urbanized region. The Central region is characterized by open plains and is largely agricultural. The mountains of the East are forested and support coal mining. The West is hilly and also largely forested, bounded on its western edge by the Ohio River as it runs into the Mississippi.

The regions are not political subunits of the state, they are comprised of about 25-40 counties each. The regions are geographically distinct, and vary in topography, resources, population, economic activity and degree of urbanization. The regional borders delineate approximate borders of these geographic regions, running along county borders for analytical convenience. The regions are distinguished to track variations in economic impacts in areas with varying primary economic activities. However, an inability to distinguish between regions, through lack of a complete economy-environment interaction rationale at the regional level, severely limited the project's ability to distinguish effects regionally in the state.

We conducted our environmental impact projections using the four regions of the state they as they are delineated in the REMI model; this is the accepted regional description for state policy makers and the REMI model gave us good social and economic regional results. However, in determining environmental effects, the regional divisions were significantly less useful. While the regions as defined are loosely bounded as geographic regions and have more or less distinct economic and social characteristics, they are not bounded as either air sheds or watersheds. For many impacts and variables, the activity-environment interactions and impacts could not be reasonably forecasted for these regions.

Some environmental variables are the same in each region, such as the rate of emissions from burning gasoline in cars. Using this as an example, a distinguished regional environmental result concerning the resultant level of air pollution would depend on the path of these pollutants. Some air pollutants, such as ground-level ozone, are sufficiently localized to regard as effectively limited to their region of origin. Others flow accordingly to environmental characteristics such as an air shed. For many environmental effects of economic activity, dispersal or accumulation occurs according to specifically environmental regions, such as air sheds or watersheds. The socioeconomic regions used in the state regional definitions did not form useful proxies for regions of environmental effect. That is, a linkage particular to a region was not determinable, in such a way that it would have been sufficient to develop a set of interaction data for the POLESTAR model.

In some cases, there was sufficient activity data to have informed an analysis of watershed or air shed effects, but the regions of the state do not correspond to watershed or air shed boundaries. Some environmental data were available that were tabulated according to another system of regions that did not correspond to the state regional coverage. The technical committees engaged in the comparative risk assessment project utilized physiographic regions, that were smaller than these four regions and which could not be converted. This limited our access to regional data on current conditions, problems and threats. In any case, these data would have had to be attributed "backwards" to regional activities using some activity-environment rationale or linkage. Another limitation on our regional environmental analysis was that much of the data that would have been needed concerning the environmental effects of current levels and types of economic activity were simply not available at the regional level.

Nonetheless, we were able distinguish some findings by region, where the data we did have projected sufficiently large divergences. There are a few fundamental and regionally specific socioeconomic and environmental differences that override the otherwise minimal data on the nuances of impacts, and that enable regional economy-environment linkages to be made. The Bluegrass Region, which contains the major urbanized areas of Louisville, Lexington, and Northern Kentucky, is vastly more urbanized than the rest of the state. The Eastern Region is projected to lose population over the next thirty years, while the rest of the state will experience population increases. Core economic activities such as coal mining and tobacco farming rank very differently in importance across the regions. And finally, the four regions were expected to experience very different effects from any shift toward increased timbering or tourism activity. These differences enabled sufficiently broad distinctions in sufficiently regionalized environmental effects to enable regional distinctions to be forecast.

Baseline and restructured projections: Imagining a different mix of economic activities

Two different economic projections for 2025 were employed in this study. Econometric models are generally assumed to be relatively accurate with respect to aggregate employment and total product for a maximum of five years, after which uncertainties rise tremendously. Thus the thirty-year estimates by the REMI econometric model for the state and its regions provide a broad-brush picture of the directions of economic change, given past trends. Such a picture is sufficient, however, for consideration of the relative magnitudes of the environmental impacts of economic activity under different scenario conditions.

For a Baseline Projection, we extrapolated the current data and inter-sector linkages in the REMI econometric model over a thirty-year time frame. Effectively, this approach assumes no major shifts in state economic development policy or in the national and global economic systems within which the state economy functions. This projection built on recent trends to project the future pattern of economic activity, and thus incorporates economic policy and development priority shifts that had already had a significant effect on the state economy.

The Restructured Projection was a constructed alternative that specified deviations from the baseline in particular sectors. It was developed from the baseline projections for this study by the staff of the Legislative Research Commission through the introduction of specific modifications, summarized in Table 5.1. In general, the restructured economy reflects possible changes in levels of economic activity in the five sectors that had been identified as the analytical priorities for this forecasting effort. The changes introduced and the rationales for them included intentional interventions in the state economy and the effects of external trends. We did not suggest that any or all of these changes were certain to take place. The Restructured Projection was an alternative future state economy that was possible. This different economy was an amalgam of changes that the economic development ministry and others were pursuing, in combination with external pressures on the economy of the state. These changes could force economic changes, whether or not the people of the state desired them.

The Restructured Projection included significant changes to the tobacco industry in the state. In this projection, we predicted a reduction in the acreage devoted to the farming of tobacco by fifty per cent over the next 30 years. This is a relatively small extension of the forty per cent decrease in the burley tobacco quota, over 10 years that had been previously examined by the LTPRC. The quotas may be expected to decline for a number of reasons, including increased burley tobacco growing overseas, and the possibility of a growing proportion of tobacco processing moving out of this state and out of the United States as a whole. Whatever the tobacco consumption patterns in the United States, global trends suggest that worldwide demand will not decline and may very well grow.

The Restructured Projection also included significant changes in the coal industry. The issue in coal mining is not resource depletion, or running out of coal. That is unlikely in the next 30 years, even at the county level. In fact, improved burning technologies could regenerate demands for the higher sulfur coal of the Western region, as well as improve the competitive position of all of the state's coal resources relative to natural gas and other alternative energy sources. Those same technologies, however, may be significantly more efficient, and enable more electricity generation per ton of coal, thus reducing the potential growth in demand for coal. As well, in consideration of the reports that were already available at the time of we made these projections, we felt that the problem of global warming was sufficiently likely to affect future decisions about energy sources. We predicted increasing concern about greenhouse gasses in general, and the carbon dioxide

88

generated by fossil fuel consumption in particular. The effect of this concern on total coal consumption might well be significant. We intentionally painted a bleak future for coal, and predicted a gradual decline of fifteen per cent in the demand for coal from both the eastern and western coalfields to be tested in the Restructured Projection.

Table 5.1
Changes assumed in the restructured economy projection

Sector	Change Introduced into REMI Projection to 2025
Tobacco and Agriculture	Reduction of 50% in burley tobacco quotas
Coal Mining	Reduction of 15% in coal mined, proportional between Eastern and Western regions
Secondary Wood Processing	Increase of 20% in lower skill and 10% in higher skill wood processing
Manufacturing Attraction and Succession	Increases in initial projections in production sectors: 5% in metal machining, 20% in machinery, 10% in automobile, 15% in plastic products
Tourism	A 7% increase in tourism, as a three million person-night increase in stays

The Restructured Economy also incorporates changes in the secondary wood-processing sector in the state. Recent years have seen a growth in wood processing in the state, especially the establishment of new of chip, strand and paper mills. The state is also pursuing the location of new installations of other forms of secondary wood processing activities. Such activities as furniture making tend to be higher skill than many other forms of wood manufacturing, and we are at a competitive disadvantage in the high skill sectors relative to locations with more skilled workers. Accordingly, we pessimistically assumed no new increases in furniture production, but we incorporated growth in the other value added wood production sectors into

89

our forecasted alternative economic future. For these other sectors, we predicted a sectoral growth rate ten to twenty per cent faster than was expected in the Baseline Economy projection.

Manufacturing attraction and succession was identified as another critical economic sector for the state, and in the Restructured Economy we predicted an improved level of performance as compared to the Baseline Economy. Without any real differences in state economic development efforts, the same forces that may reduce demands for coal may well increase manufacturing activity in the state. The strongest effects might be felt in sectors that produce products with high volume to value ratios. For products in these sectors, transportation cost is a significant concern in selecting plant or production locations. Increasing concern over energy use and carbon dioxide generation would be likely to drive up transportation costs. Higher transportation costs, especially in these transportation cost-sensitive manufacturing businesses, would increasingly favor production locales that are centralized in relation to distribution networks. This would favor the state of Kentucky. Accordingly, we forecast a five per cent increase in metal machining and related work and twenty per cent in machinery production.

The state's central position in the new "auto alley" of automobile manufacturing may be a lead factor in shaping this prospect. However, our machining and machinery forecasts and our forecast of only a ten per cent increase in automobile production had to be balanced by consistency with other elements in the Restructured Economy narrative. The benefit in automobile manufacturing and related production, largely due to increasing transportation and fuel costs, could well be tempered by reduced automobile use if concerns about air pollution rise. As well, car component production may also shift from metal parts to more plastics, as vehicle weight continues to become more of a concern in pursuit of fuel efficiency. At the same time coal, a feedstock for petrochemicals, would be likely to fall in price. At the same time, the continued growth of the health care sector in Kentucky may help stimulate local production of medical supplies and devices, as it has done in other areas of medical service concentration. Overall, we felt that the Restructured Economy projection would be consistent with a fifteen per cent increase in plastic products manufacturing.

The Tourism sector would be likely to experience some of the largest regional readjustments in the Restructured Economy projection. We could assume that the other sectoral readjustments in the Restructured Economy projection would be proportional to past levels of activity in the four regions of the state. However, a strong push to stimulate tourism would have different effects regionally because of differences in the facilities available in the areas, and in the attractions that draw people to different parts of the state.

The Baseline Economy projection already included a sharply upward trend in tourism in the Bluegrass Region due to improvements in urban convention facilities. However, in the Restructured Economy we made allowances for expanded long term stays around the lakes in the West, improved prospects for ecotourism in the mountains of the East, and agrotourism around the Bluegrass. These increases would be expected in accordance with changing tastes in tourism and the increased expense of international and long-distance tourism. The regions of the state would see a higher proportion of visits from in-state tourists and from those from the surrounding states. The driving factor ratio in tourism-generated economic activity is the expenditures generated by the number of visitors. The number of visitors is translated into more food and drink sold, more sports events, fairs and attractions admissions, and so on. We adjusted the driving factors proportionally across the state, given no region-specific information with which to more specifically tailor the projected restructuring.

The Baseline Economy and the Restructured Economy projections gave us two broadly different projections for the state. The first was an extrapolation that already included the structural readjustments of the last two decades. The Restructured Economy incorporated changes in attitudes, tastes and expenditure patterns that would further alter the state economy. Some of these changes reflected increased environmentalism and changes in health behavior; many reflected increasing energy costs. Overall, these changes would be in accord with global energy costs and concerns over global warming that could well occur in the next decades. The next step in our process was to evaluate the overall environmental impact of these two paths, for a comparison.

POLESTAR scenarios: Technology, policy and behavior change and the environment

Whatever the levels of population and economic activity, the underlying factors shaping the impact of a population on the environment are shaped by choices. Different technologies, policies and behaviors, as they embody choices made by the society and by individuals, can modify the environmental consequences of population growth and productive efforts. The specific impacts of population and production are modified through linkages specific to technology, policy and behavior. In order to compare the effects of these modifiers, we developed and compared four distinct scenarios for each of the two economic projections examined.

Table 5.2
Changes assumed in the technical change scenario

Sector and Element	Changes Assumed
Transportation	Fuel efficiency rises 25%, per unit emissions fall 20%, and use of natural gas as fuel triples
Households	Lighting and appliance electricity use falls 40% For space heat, more efficient devices, change in fuels, total fuel use drops 20% For water heat, solar and exchanger replace half electric share
Service Sector	Total electricity consumption falls by 50%.
Manufacturing	Except transport fuel, industrial power use falls 30% In most sectors, biomass replaces 20-25% of fuel, heavier declines in electricity and petroleum, coal remains steady where used Chemical feedstocks set at 2% natural gas, 48% petroleum and 50% coal
Land Use	Per capita area of built environment falls, more in urban (25%) than in rural regions (10-15%) Area of forest lands grow accordingly
Solid Waste	Household waste falls by 10% due to reductions in packaging, a 6% reduction in total volume overall

We developed four scenarios in accordance with judgments about possibility. In the construction of this set of technology, policy and practice scenarios, we consulted a variety of sources to shape our assumptions. We needed to develop scenarios that were informed about trends in technological developments, and possible or likely shifts in policies and practices. The changes assumed in these scenarios were constructed from a synthesis of a broad array of material dealing with ecological, technological, regulatory and environmental attitude and behavior trends. We relied on others' forecasts and trends analyses, including those of the LTPRC. A narrower body of sources provided specific numeric data or indications of levels and speeds, not just directions, of changes. These materials shaped the specific numerical assumptions in the change scenarios. These sources had key data that helped us to quantify changes for the purpose of our analysis, for particular sectors or economic issues.

Another body of sources, mostly documentary, but partially electronic and also derived for us by state government personnel from other evidence, was critical to calibrating the POLESTAR model. Unless we had sufficient state-specific information, we refrained from providing any projections of possible environmental impacts even where POLESTAR produced some numeric results.

The four scenarios we developed are called the Status Quo, the Technological Change, the Policy and Practice Change and the Combined Change. In the Status Quo Scenario, no significant shifts in technology, regulatory practice, production techniques or patterns of consumption were envisioned, beyond those evident in current trends. This implies that the technical relationships between levels of economic activity of different kinds and their environmental consequences are projected to be effectively unchanged from those that now exist. In the model, the environmental consequences measured included such variables as emissions, wastes, resource consumption, energy generation and use, and the land required for infrastructure and other uses. The scenario made use of data obtained from state offices and agencies and other sources concerning the current levels of these impacts. Using this data, we projected 2025 conditions, based on changes in the population and economic activity in the state.

The Status Quo scenario made a reasonable match with the Baseline Projection, but it made less sense in combination with the Restructured Economy. The Restructured Economy already incorporated some changes in taste, behavior and relative prices. It also involved significant changes in land use and other variables that could affect future environmental conditions even in the absence of technological changes or shifts in consumption tastes or regulations. Given decreased reliance on tobacco farming, increased demand for forestry yields as inputs to secondary wood processing industries, decreased mining activity and increases in manufacturing and tourism, we modified the technical conditions characterizing the Status Quo under the Restructured Economy.

Whether we examined the Baseline Economy or the Restructured Economy as the projected economy in 2025, the Status Quo scenario for environmental impacts was fundamentally unrealistic. Because it assumed no change in applied technologies, regulations, or behavior by economic actors, it was the most pessimistic possible forecast of environmental conditions. In effect, it assumed an irrational commitment to "doing things the old way" in the face of new opportunities or evidence that such behaviors had undesirable effects. If there were economically viable new technologies that reduced the negative effects of production on the environment, it would be irrational not to adopt them. We should expect that they would, in fact, be accepted. Similarly, if people and firms — and regulatory agencies — discover that certain behaviors or patterns of land use, resource consumption or disposal have negative effects on them, and it is possible to change, then new behaviors and/or regulations should be expected. The more realistic scenario involves some mix of the adoption of new technologies and new modes of behavior.

Table 5.3
Changes assumed in the policy and practices scenario

Sector and Element	*Changes Assumed*
Transportation	Auto miles driven fall by 15% urban, 2-7% rural Bus travel rises to 18% of all travel urban, 2-7% rural
Households	Energy use falls by 20%, proportionately across forms
Service Sector	Energy use falls by 20%, proportionately across forms
Manufacturing	Energy use falls by 10%, proportionately across forms
Land Use	Per capita area of built environment falls by 20% urban, rises by 0-5% in rural regions Area of forest lands respond
Solid Waste	Total per capita generation falls 15% Recycling rises to 60% of generated

In the Technological Change scenario, it was assumed that engineering changes would be adopted. These included changes in production techniques and in the household goods and services that appeared to be either currently possible or potentially available within thirty years. There is a range of technological changes in the works or already on-line that were not yet broadly implemented that could have significant impact. Our assumption here was that the changes would be sufficiently attractive economically, as well as environmentally, to result in broad adoption of the new technology. Accordingly, in the Technological Change scenario we incorporated changes that included: improved vehicular fuel efficiency and emissions, improved insulation and heating efficiency in homes, improved and more efficient appliances and lighting, shifts in energy utilization from fossil fuels other than coal toward renewable sources, and reductions in the land per capita needed for infrastructure and the built environment. Table 5.2 summarizes the technological shifts we incorporated into this scenario.

Technological advance would not depend on any particular action within the state. It is possible that the modification of some regulatory practices could accelerate the acceptance and distribution of such developments. These changes in how we produce and consume can thus shape environmental impacts even in the absence of any changes in the policies, practices, tastes or behaviors of the people of the state.

We developed another scenario that focused on changes in behaviors and policy. The Policy and Practices Change scenario assumed that changes would occur in public and private practices and expectations. Through a combination of strong leadership favoring sustainable development and increasing evidence of threats or damage to the environment, a new level of concern would be generated. Under this scenario, this concern was translated into changes in policies and behaviors. The result would modify the impacts of a given level of activity on future environmental conditions.

In this case, we assumed no change to the technologies available, but an increased reliance on those technologies and behavioral changes associated with higher levels of environmental literacy. These changes included, for example, a higher rate of use of mass transit, lowered electricity use and increased rates of recycling. In addition, we assumed improvements in the public infrastructure for environmental protection including sewer and water systems, transportation systems, and other public investments. These changes in tastes, policies, and practices are summarized in Table 5.3.

Both the Technological Change and the Policies and Practices Change scenarios made use of the key context variables developed with the advisory group. For the highest ranked item, Environmental Literacy, the premise was that a better understanding of environmental processes and of the risks associated with human economic activity would lead to greater willingness to act to reduce negative impacts and to accept regulations that protected the environment. One very strong effect of this willingness to act would be increased household recycling. Effects could also include increased demand for more efficient household products and attitude changes that would lead to reduced environmental impacts. For example, retailers might reduce lighting levels, reducing energy demand and also emissions from power generation.

95

Table 5.4
Changes assumed in the combined change scenario

Sector and Element   *Changes Assumed*

Transportation   Fuel efficiency rises by 25%, per unit emissions fall by
20%, and use of natural gas as fuel triples
Auto miles driven fall by 15% urban, 0-5% rural
Bus travel rises to 18% of all travel urban, 2-7% rural

Households   Lighting and appliance electricity use falls 40%
For space heat, more efficient devices, change in fuels,
total fuel use drops 20%
For water heat, solar and exchanger replace half electric
share

Service Sector   Total energy use falls by 20%, proportionately across
forms of energy other than electricity
Electricity usage falls by 50%
Emissions per unit of fuel falls by 20%

Manufacturing   Total energy use falls by 30%, proportionately across
all forms of energy other than petroleum
In most sectors, biomass replaces 20-25% of fuel,
heavier declines in electricity and petroleum, coal
remains steady where used
Chemical feedstocks set at 2% natural gas, 48%
petroleum and 50% coal

Land Use   Per capita built environment required falls 25% urban,
10% rural
Forest land area grows in response

Solid Waste   Total per capita generation falls 20%
Recycling rises to 60% of all generated

The pursuit of more Sustainable Development was the next key context variable. An increase in the sustainability of economic development efforts might be efficient in monetary as well as environmental terms, since the likelihood of a threat to continued activity is reduced. The policy concern involved a recognition that some activities simply would not be possible. The non-attainment status of areas of the state under the Clean Air Act, whatever the reasons for that status, is at least an indication of potential problems in sustaining a given growth path. For the Bluegrass Region in particular, technological changes that reduce emissions were incorporated. In the practice scenario, behavioral changes were incorporated such as an acute reduction in the use of gasoline-fired activity.

The Need for Leadership context variable was certainly relevant to the search for alternatives and options in pursuit of sustainable economic development. Given our findings, appropriate leadership must recognize the potential to pursue stimuli for the generation and adoption of environment-conserving technological change, especially when such changes do not add to the cost of goods and services or reduce profits. At the same time, leadership must also recognize that an effort to incorporate conserving technologies should not involve the weakening of current environmental protection policies, regulations, and practices.

A Public Works investment in the state holds the promise of reducing negative environmental impacts through the adoption of the most advanced technologies. In our scenarios, these technologies included new means of providing mass transportation and reducing automobile use. Communications infrastructure investments could, conceivably, help shift the state economy towards types of employment and production that minimize negative environmental effects within the state. The ability of our project to investigate this issue in detail was severely impaired by the incomplete data available on water uses and contamination problems in the state and the inability to deal with water issues in the POLESTAR modeling effort.

New technologies affected the Energy Use Changes context variable, and can play very important roles in shaping both the state economy and its environmental impacts. Shifting demands for coal may be associated with its use for generating energy. Energy production and consumption accounted for the largest part of the air pollutants discussed here. Any technological or taste changes that alter the use of, and emissions from, different energy generators will produce significant environmental effects. As well, the substitution of less acutely polluting biomass sources for fossil hydrocarbons in the generation of electricity could have major impacts. Effective air pollution controls appear to be necessary for continuation of much of the current economic development.

Finally, we developed one further prospective scenario, which we called the Combined Change scenario. In Combined Change, the effects of technological changes are combined with shifts in household, company, and public sector tastes and practices. These changes are all directionally in ways that reduce adverse environmental impacts. However, some of the changes in technology may be driven by changes in tastes, or, alternatively, technological advances may make particular behavioral objectives or desired practices easier to attain. Therefore, the combination of the two change trends was not a simple summation of the other two. In some instances, the combined percentage change effect was a multiple of the two isolated effects. In other cases, a reduced environmental impact objective may be met by one or another trend alone, and no more change may occur. In this instance, the combined change may be no more than the larger of the two effects in the isolated scenarios. The Combined Change shifts are summarized in Table 5.4.

At this point in our forecasting effort, we had developed two economic projections and four scenarios. Both the projections and the scenarios responded to the advisory group process, in that the priority economic sectors and certain elements of the priority environmental analysis had been used to form the scenarios and projections and to inform our attempts at data collection and impact analysis. We had also attempted to develop the scenarios and the models according to the findings about environmental impact priorities that had been developed in the advisory group process. However, the scenarios and projections could only incorporate analysis of a smaller set of priorities than the advisory group had identified. While water quality and waste treatment had been identified as a priority policy context area, our ability to model water quality was particularly limited by the difficulty in linking the economic activity and the existing data into their environmental impacts. Our best linkage data was for air quality; the extent to which this analysis could be regionally distinguished was also limited.

Our scenarios did not include any analysis of radical environmental impact or catastrophe. Such a scenario might have included such elements as a sharp increase in unpredictable weather due to global warming, a massive influx of environmental refugees, global political insecurity and an associated economic depression. Again, our choices of projections and scenarios were tailored to our policy audience. We wanted to develop scenarios that had the potential to affect current policy choices. We needed to engage this particular audience and, if possible, challenge complacency about the sustainability of the status quo, projected rather simply. The scenarios we developed were suitable for this purpose. The next step was to develop our analysis of the environmental impacts of these relatively peaceful futures.

6 Comparing the effects of economic activity, technologies and practices on environmental impacts

Once the scenarios were generated and described, they could be compared. First, we analyzed the Baseline Status Quo, the scenario that seemed to involve the least change in current economic paths, technologies, and policies and behaviors. This described a future of relatively rapid economic growth with serious environmental impacts. In consideration of existing laws and national policies that are likely to impact the state, we demonstrated that the Baseline Status Quo was not actually very likely. Certain impacts, such as certain measures of air quality, are already limitations to the economic growth of the area; the costs of these and other impacts would be likely to rise in the future, and arrest the ability of the area to develop economically. Change is not only likely, and inadequate change is likely to have economic effects.

The Restructured Projection and the alternative scenarios are based on changes in five priority economic sectors. The five sectors were those identified by the advisory group for priority consideration: energy with an emphasis on coal, manufacturing promotion and succession, production agriculture with a focus on tobacco, tourism, and value-added wood processing. The Restructured Projection posits alternative futures for these sectors. These futures appear possible given external pressures and state economic development priorities. The scenarios focus on changes relevant to these sectors as well as to the five priorities identified by the advisory group. For the sake of simplicity, the Restructured Projection ignored possible changes in less important sectors (see Table 5.1).

Our first task was to describe the outlines of the Baseline Status Quo scenario. Then, we undertook a pairwise comparison of the other projections. We scanned some of the major differences between the forecasts associated with the Status Quo and Combined Change scenarios for the Baseline Projection. Then, we compared the Status Quo and Combined Change scenarios for the Restructured Projection. The comparison that was most interesting was between the Baseline Status Quo and the Restructured Combined Change.

Finally, we considered how much of the differences between the Baseline Status Quo and the Restructured Combined Change were due to technology change, and how much to regulations or education. Technology change is not feasibly controlled or developed by state efforts alone, although the state can require that certain kinds of existing technologies be used or implemented. The state does have control over the level of environmental regulations and education. The input of the project advisory group concerning the priority on environmental literacy and the likelihood of behavioral changes in the population both come into focus in this section.

The baseline economy projection: Can past trends continue?

The Baseline Economy, projected using the REMI model, shows that the state economy, if it continues along the path that it is currently following, will grow by forty-seven per cent in total output by the year 2025. With population expanding by only five per cent, this translates into a forty per cent increase in per capita income, measured in constant purchasing power. However, Table 6.1 shows that the increased economic well being of the state is accompanied by continued deterioration of the natural environment.

The increase in pollutants is not proportional to the increase in GDP or in total energy consumption. The Baseline Economy under the Status Quo scenario includes some efficiency and pollution abatement trends already underway. For example, the annual release of volatile organic compounds (VOCs) rises by only seven per cent; this reflects the fleet upgrade that occurs as older more polluting engines are phased out. As well, certain types of pollutant releases are constrained in the Baseline Status Quo scenario through existing regulations; this explains the less than proportional increase in releases of sulfur dioxide. It is important to remember that some of the environmental impacts of economic activity occur elsewhere; these "pollutant exports" occur mainly through the purchase of electric power generated out-of-state. These exported emissions or other environmental impacts are not reflected in the total emissions and releases listed in Table 6.1.

Table 6.1
Changes in conditions, 2025: Baseline, status quo scenario

Economic or Environmental Condition	The Condition After 30 Years	
	Total Level	Percentage Change
Gross Domestic Product (GDP)	$111,000,000,000	47%
Population	4,000,000	5%
GDP per Person	$27,750	40%
Annual Total Energy Consumed	2,073 Petajoules	44%
Annual Carbon Dioxide Emissions	278 Megatons	17%
Annual Releases of Sulfur Dioxide	914 Kilotons	12%
Annual Volatile Organic Compounds	1104 Kilotons	7%

Totals for the state, however, mask some serious problems in the regions, where impacts are unequal. The fastest growth is expected to occur in the urbanized Bluegrass. This region shows a 54 per cent increase in gross domestic product (GDP) and an 18 per cent increase in population. While population is expected to remain almost unchanged in the Western and Central regions, it is projected to decline by 12 per cent in the East. The East has the lowest growth in GDP, at 32 per cent.

The Baseline Status Quo scenario results underscore a weakness of any econometric model; the inability to incorporate trend reversals or shifts in the future. All the model can do is extrapolate from past trends, albeit with some sophistication. New constraints, and opportunities cannot be incorporated into the model unless they have become visible in the recent past as emerging trends. Most significantly, such models cannot account for rapid, unexpected, one-time events. For example, the location of a large manufacturing plant in one of the rural areas of the state can have large impacts that cannot be modelled. Similarly, the effects of events such as earthquakes or tornadoes cannot be predicted. The longer the timeframe projected using econometric models, the less reliable past trends become in generating forecasts.

With little recent population change in the West and Central regions, the model predicted no change over the next thirty years. In effect, this assumed some outmigration, since the population would naturally increase with births outnumbering deaths as they still do in most of the United States. Other shifts were more interesting. On a per capita income basis, the East was predicted to catch up to the Bluegrass despite lower total income gains. This shift was due to population loss in the East, largely through outmigration, and major gains in numbers of residents in the Bluegrass.

Total energy use was projected to rise proportionately to total GDP under the Status Quo Scenario. The forty four per cent increase in GDP resulted in a forty four per cent gain in total energy use. Petroleum and total electricity showed increases that were also nearly proportional, reflecting a nearly constant share as energy sources. The share of energy demand sourced from natural gas decreased substantially, while the share sourced from coal increased substantially. There was an overall 86 per cent increase in the demand for coal, reflecting its larger role in supplying energy needs in the state, in electricity generation in the Central region in particular. In all our scenarios, coal's share of the energy source total rose 20 per cent or more. This is good news for the coal industry in the state. However, the data on the state reliance on coal reflects the interest of the state government in using its resources. There would be no reason to expect a similar increase in the export (non-state) utilization of coal. This might mean that the total demand for coal produced in the state would fall, even if internal use rose.

However, the rise in overall energy demand at the same rate as total GDP rises does not reflect the likelihood of increased developments in technological efficiency. We have ample evidence of downward trends in the energy used per dollar of output. Energy demand cannot be reasonably expected to increase at the same rate as GDP; it is far more likely that it would increase at a slightly lower rate to reflect marginal further increases in efficiency and conservation.

Current trends projected forward raise suggest serious environmental concerns, the extent of which raises doubt about our ability to continue in the current patterns. Our project was able to calculate projected increases in both greenhouse gas emissions and ground-level emissions. Regulations already penalize the current levels of ground-level emissions without increase, and it is likely that greenhouse gas emissions will be increasingly regulated over the next three decades. Greenhouse gas emission increases, shown regionally in Figure 6.1, would be about thirty per cent in total. In the Central region where increased electricity generation was forecast, the resultant increase in carbon dioxide emissions would be over fifty per cent. Increasingly, as global warming becomes a policy issue at the national and international levels, the state is likely to face a major problem. As coherent action is undertaken to reduce outputs that contribute to the phenomenon, energy solutions that suit some of the objectives of the state may not be possible. These might include limitations on the projected use of coal in electricity generation in the Central region; the implications of that might entail increased energy costs for the state as a whole.

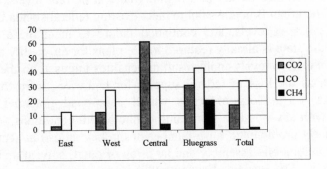

Figure 6.1 Change in greenhouse gas emissions, 1995-2025: Baseline projection, status quo scenario

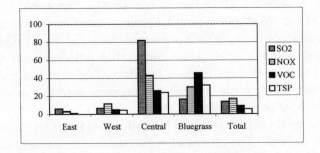

Figure 6.2 Change in ground level emissions, 1995-2025: Baseline projection, status quo scenario

Whether or not a global policy solution is emerging to reduce or control greenhouse gas emissions, the projected increase in ground-level pollutants in the Bluegrass would not be possible under existing Federal law.[1] The noxious odor of the nitrous oxide may be an annoyance, but it can have serious health consequences, as can the particulate matter (TSP), which is

103

taken into the lungs through the act of breathing. Of central concern, Figure 6.2 shows a 43 per cent increase in the Bluegrass in volatile organic compounds (VOC). VOCs are released by gas and diesel fueled vehicles and by a broad cross-section of manufacturing activities. They are a key element in smog and a factor in ozone generation, and have demonstrated negative health effects. The projected increases in VOCs emissions would jeopardize the health of citizens living and working in the affected areas. Furthermore, the projected increase occurs in a region where at current levels, significant portions of the urban Bluegrass fail to meet existing federal standards.

Current emission levels, and continued failure to meet these standards, means that the state is already required to file plans for air quality attainment. Worsening emission levels could result in penalties imposed on the state as a whole, such as the loss of federal support for highways, infrastructure and other grants. This loss of funds would compound potential problems associated with any possible worsening public health conditions. Emissions are particularly problematic for a number of the key industrial sectors in the Bluegrass: automobile assembly and an array of paint, solvent and chemical manufacturing. The Baseline Economy thus ignores a major constraint to the continuation of past trends and may, in effect, prove to be unattainable.

Major impacts may be very concentrated in narrow geographic areas of the state. Very different effects may be expected across the four broad regions of the state on the basis of population change alone. The projected 5 per cent increase in population statewide is not evenly distributed. While the population of the West and central Regions is more or less unchanged, the East will experience a 13 per cent population drop and the Bluegrass will see its population climb 17 per cent. Substantial differences in the impacts experienced in these two regions may be attributable to this migration pattern alone, regardless of growth in levels of economic activity per capita or the types of economic changes that take place.

One of the most obvious facets of humankind's impact on the environment is in the use of land. The effects of economic activity on land use are most obvious in the Bluegrass. With its 17 per cent increase in population, urbanized land area would be expected to increase by 18 per cent in accordance with current land consumption patterns. Accordingly, the Bluegrass would see declines in the land devoted to crops, pastures and forests.

While the Eastern Region shows a substantial drop in population, it would not show a comparable shift in land use patterns. The land use variable of concern is the transformation of land from farms, woodlot, and open space into the human "built environment" of roads, other public infrastructure, homes and businesses. Over a thirty-year time period, the portions of the

104

built environment that would be abandoned by an outmigrant population in the East would not have reverted to more natural land forms. By contrast, the exceptional growth in population in the Bluegrass would result in an expansion of the built environment.

The key assumption in the Baseline Status Quo scenario land use projections is that land use patterns would continue as they are now. New development and the expansion of infrastructure would be proportional to population growth, and would transform rural land to urbanized land at current rates. Whatever changes in the structure of the economy would occur, they would not affect the amount of built environment used per capita. In this scenario, the possibility that older, existing, or potentially underutilized built environment could be redeveloped at greater rates than current has not been incorporated. Abandoned and underutilized real estate already exists in urban centers, and it is probable that ways will be found to use it in the future. The "current pattern continues" assumption is not really tenable. As well, the inability to account for "one-time" events, such as new park or protected area set-asides draws attention to the inability of the model to incorporate likely policy actions.

These assumptions highlight the need to consider other projections and scenarios. They help to illustrate our point that a "no change" or Status Quo Scenario forward for thirty years is fundamentally unrealistic. The reason is that we include a Baseline Status Quo scenario for analysis is that, despite its faults, it gives us a starting point from which to work in building alternative scenarios. It becomes the foundation for the introduction of the changes that constitute the other scenarios. It also illustrates, quite graphically, the outcomes of a "do nothing" approach — and the effective impossibility of standing still. In this sense, our starting point, the Baseline Economy and the Status Quo scenario, with no changes, is unduly pessimistic. This is good, but it also means that the improvements to be gained from the technological changes and shifts in tastes, practices, and policies we consider in the other scenarios are not as great as the data here seem to indicate.

Next, we compare the Baseline Status Quo Scenario with a Restructured Combined Change Scenario. The Restructured Combined Change reflects the Restructured Economy in combination with both technological changes and changes in tastes, policies, and practices of households and businesses. The significance of this comparison would be invisible had we not reported the findings of the Status Quo Scenario, unrealistic as they may be. Using the Baseline Status Quo, we can trace a substantial departure associated with allowing change to occur under market and regulatory pressures and non-market preference changes. Accepting the more realistic scenario incorporating changes, we find a reduction in the land area covered by the

105

built environment. We also find major improvements in energy efficiency. Nevertheless, even the changes associated with the Restructured Combined Change Scenario would not substantially slow growth in energy demand throughout the state. Under the Combined Change Scenario, the use of petroleum for generating electricity would decline, as would the quantity of electricity generated by fossil fuels, allowing for some reliance on biomass.

We have not discussed the costs that may be incurred by the state or by the economy of any technological or political changes, or of the cost of doing nothing. To the extent that changes may be relatively cost-free or borne by out-of-state consumers of in-state products and services, the alternative course of action would become more preferable. All the projections of the growth of the market for new and improved environmental technologies are expected to expand rapidly, perhaps doubling in the next decade. The state is already engaged in exporting such technologies, so any potential for expansion in this market would strengthen the case for public sector spending to stimulate technology change promotion.

Adjusting for probable and possible change

Our next step was the analysis of how changes in technologies available, and in the tastes, policies, and practices of households and businesses, could affect the impact of the state's continued economic expansion on its environment. We begun by scanning some major differences between the forecasts associated with the Status Quo and Combined Change Scenarios for the Baseline Projection. We then made similar comparisons, between the Status Quo and Combined Change Scenario for the Restructured projections.

Land use projections differed markedly between the Status Quo and the Combined Change scenarios. The Combined Change scenario predicted that significantly less land would be required per capita for new development in the built environment. As well, the scenario predicted the rapid rehabilitation of idle, previously developed non-urban land to productive forestry. Introducing these possibilities through the Combined Change scenario, significant shifts in land consumption would occur. Figure 6.3 illustrates the possible effects of a reduction in the extent of the built environment used by the people of the state as a whole.

Such a shift could be explained through different motivations, it could occur for a variety of reasons. It is possible that people would want to reduce or minimize the time and expense of commuting by relocating closer to where they work, perhaps for reasons of family time or due to rising costs. If many households wanted to lower their individual commutes, they might choose to live at slightly higher densities (people per acre). The reclamation and reuse of previously developed and currently underutilized urban sites might occur in response to this demand. In centrally located neighborhoods this might take the form of urban infill, gentrification, renovation of existing houses or even lot assembly and new building construction.

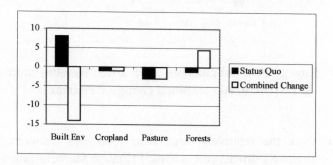

Figure 6.3   Kentucky land use change, 1995-2025: Baseline projection, status quo vs. combined change scenarios

Outside of the city, the Combined Change land use pattern would predict more attention to reforestation, both on existing forest lands and on the reclamation of abandoned non-urban lands. This could occur due to new demands for a larger variety of raw materials for wood processing industries. It might also occur through recognition that forests help clean the local air, and might allow more local emissions. The combination of these behavioral and technological changes can make a substantial difference.

Emissions would also change substantially as a result of the changes in technologies and tastes, practices, and regulations we hypothesized. The Combined Change scenario showed major improvements over the Status Quo in energy efficiency as the result of the changes we hypothesized. When we compare the changes in total energy demand between the Baseline Status Quo to the Restructured Combined Change, we saw considerable energy savings, illustrated in Figure 6.4. In both scenarios there was a shift in energy generating effort, and therefore in total local energy demand toward the Central region. This shift suggests that an increasing proportion of electrical energy will be supplied through coal-fired generators in the Central region, as in recent years. This shift might have serious implications for air quality. However, the adverse effects are muted by lower total energy demand under the Restructured Combined Change scenario.

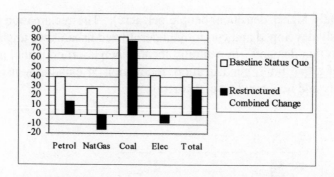

Figure 6.4   Energy demand changes, 1995-2025: Baseline status quo vs. restructured combined change scenarios

However, even the relatively large behavioral and technological shifts associated with the Restructured Combined Change scenario failed to rein in power demands, which still rose 22 per cent in total. Energy use still increased, in the state as a whole, and in all the regions except the East. Moreover, a 2 per cent decline in the eastern region was projected under the Combined Change Scenario in which population in the region would fall by over 13 per cent. Energy consumption per capita in the East was still predicted to grow by about 12 per cent under the Combined Change Scenario.

What did change in the shift to the Combined Change Scenario is the composition of the energy used. Allowing for some reliance on biomass fuels, we found a decrease in the quantity of fossil fuels used in electricity generation. As well, there was a decreased use of petroleum for purposes other than electricity generation.

The exploration of the economic projections and the scenarios revealed several important findings. First, under the Baseline Projection and the Status Quo Scenario, the state economy would grow substantially over the next 30 years, other things being equal. Second, this growth is likely to carry a heavy price in the form of increased release of both greenhouse gasses and ground-level emissions. Third, since the impact of this projected increase in emissions would be most pronounced in the Bluegrass and Central regions, the projected growth may be unattainable. The desired increases in income per person may not be attainable simply through a sacrifice of environmental conditions to economic expansion. Fourth, in the Bluegrass Region, increases in population and economic growth would cause a further shift in land use patterns with more land converted from crops, pasture, and forests to the built environment. Finally, in the state, the demand for and utilization of coal for the generation of power and other energy uses may well expand in the future. All of these findings must be viewed in light of the fact that the status quo scenario we have defined is highly unrealistic because it assumes no change whatsoever in either relevant technologies or in behaviors and practices that may affect environmental conditions.

The environmental consequences of economic restructuring

Compared to the Baseline, the Restructured Projection involved an expansion in the production of wood products and other manufacturing. Tourism promotion was more successful, for a variety of reasons including shorter trip distances by out of state tourists. However, there was a need to adapt to reduced demands for tobacco and coal. Under Status Quo conditions for the Restructured economy, GDP would have grown by 49 per cent by the year 2025, 2 per cent more than the Baseline Status Quo scenario. With population expanding by only 5 per cent, this translated into a 42 per cent increase in per capita income, measured in constant purchasing power. Again, as in the case of the Baseline Projection, these changes have their price in deterioration of the natural environment in the state. Table 6.2 compares the performance of the Baseline to the Restructured Projections under the Status Quo scenario.

Under the Status Quo scenario, there seems to be a sharper tradeoff between the environment and economic gain in the Restructured than in the Baseline Projection. That is, the Restructured economy appears to generate a bit more in GDP per capita. However, it also shows a worsening in a number of key environmental measures, such as air pollutants released and energy consumed. Carbon dioxide emissions would be higher, and carbon dioxide is a greenhouse gas. Sulfur dioxide would be released in larger quantities; this is the most common substance that makes the air smell bad. Releases of volatile organic compounds (VOCs) that are the basis for the elevated levels of ozone in the major urban centers of the state would even get a bit worse. Again, considering that at current emissions levels there are "nonattainment areas" already in violation of existing national air quality standards, such deterioration poses a serious problem in the future.

While the state-level aggregate showed economic gains, these were not evenly distributed. Under the Restructured economy, the gains in tourism, manufacturing and timbering do not compensate adequately for the loss in coal employment income, although they do seem to cover the loss of tobacco acreage. Compared to the Baseline Projection, there are GDP gains for all the regions of the state except the East. The Eastern region also suffers increased population outmigration as a result. The outmigration contributed to more severe negative environmental changes in the already strained Bluegrass, the region closest to the East. The Restructured Projection under the Status Quo scenario would also be substantially more energy intensive than the Baseline economy; the Restructured Status Quo results in a GDP that is 5 per cent higher, but total energy demand rises 13 per cent.

Table 6.2
Changes in conditions, 2025:
Baseline and restructured projections, status quo scenario

Economic or Environmental Condition	The State of the Condition After 30 Years	
	Baseline Projection	Restructured Projection
Gross Domestic Product	$111,000,000,000	$116,000,000,000
Population	4,000,000	4,000,000
GDP per Person	$27,750	$29,000
Annual Total Energy Consumed	2,073 Petajoules	2,347 Petajoules
Annual Carbon Dioxide Emissions	278 Megatons	296 Megatons
Annual Releases of Sulfur Dioxide	914 Kilotons	966 Kilotons
Annual Volatile Organic Compounds	1,104 Kilotons	1,116 Kilotons

The move to coal shown in the Restructured Projection, while potentially beneficial to the economies of the coal regions, would not be without its problems. As Figures 6.5 and 6.6 indicate, all the major elements of air pollution would rise more rapidly in a Status Quo move to a Restructured economy. For the Baseline, we had noted very high regional concentrations of increases in greenhouse gas emissions projected for the Central Region (carbon dioxide and sulfur dioxide) and an increase in poisonous carbon monoxide in the Bluegrass; these were displayed in Figures 6.1 and 6.2. The

Restructured Status Quo economy would imply even greater releases concentrated in those areas. The human health effects of these greater concentrated releases would probably mean that the releases would not be permissible. Whether this violation would limit the activity or require greater control expenses is not clear.

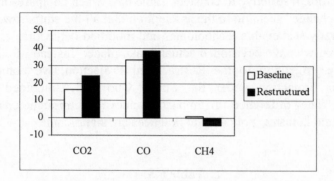

Figure 6.5   Change in greenhouse gas emissions, 1995-2025:
Baseline vs. restructured projections, status quo scenario

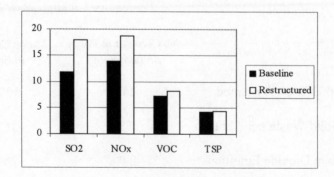

Figure 6.6   Total ground level emissions, 1995-2025:
Baseline vs. restructured projections, status quo scenario

However, there is an important problem with these findings for the Restructured Economy under the Status Quo. The projections assumed only those technological, attitudinal, behavioral or regulatory changes that were already evident in 1995. This assumption is hard to defend even for the

111

Baseline Projection, as we have noted. The "no change" scenario becomes totally untenable for the Restructured Projection. It is highly probable that the forces that might shape an economy with less coal mining, more tourism and manufacturing, more effective use of forest products and reduced acres committed to tobacco will also alter both technology used in the state and the environmental behaviors of state households and businesses.

It is, therefore, instructive to consider Table 6.3, which compares the Status Quo or "no change" scenario to the assumption that all the shifts toward more environmentally sustainable technologies and modified behaviors, values and regulation that we have envisioned actually take place. Instead of comparing the Baseline Projection to the Restructured Projection, we compare the Restructured Projection under the Status Quo and Combined Change scenarios. The difference in impacts achievable through changes in technology and in tastes, policies and practices are significant.

Table 6.3
Changes in conditions, 2025:
Restructured projection, status quo and combined change

Economic or Environmental Condition	Restructured Projection Conditions: Percentage Changes from 1995	
	No Changes in Policy or Technology	Major Changes in Both
Annual Total Energy Consumed	44%	15%
Municipal Solid Waste per Annum	5%	-16%
Annual Carbon Dioxide Emissions	24%	7%
Annual Releases of Sulfur Dioxide	18%	14%
Annual Volatile Organic Compounds	8%	10%

While the improvements between scenarios are significant, the overall picture that emerges is not encouraging. With the restructuring of the state economy in directions that seem probable at this point and would normally be considered to benefit the environment, conditions do not improve over those

112

we see at the present time. The Restructured Combined Change has incorporated environmentally preserving technologies. As well, it includes value shifts that generate more pro-conservation decisions and actions by businesses and household. It has also included regulatory practices that encourage or require such behavior changes. Still, it appears that things generally will get worse from an environmental perspective, even if only by as little as 7 per cent, given economic strategies currently considered to be viable.

The one exception in the picture of overall poorer environmental performance is in the measure of solid waste generated. Municipal solid waste could be reduced by regulatory and behavioral change, to 16 per cent below its current level. While important, a reduction in solid waste has fewer long-term impacts for global sustainability. If solid waste were to increase, it would require only the conversion of more lands to landfills. Non-toxic solid wastes will not threaten human health in the ways that climate change, air pollution and contaminated lands and water could. It is even possible that widespread household attention, time and energy devoted to waste reduction actually reduces the amount attention, time and energy devoted to changing production and consumption habits that are far more damaging to the global environment.

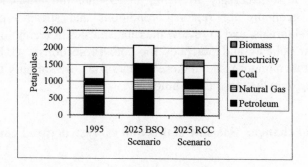

Figure 6.7   Possible changes in energy demand and composition

Another partial bright spot is energy use. Total usage clearly continues to rise as compared to the present. However, the increase is very significantly reduced, from 44 per cent to 15 per cent, as illustrated in Figure 6.7. Moreover, the composition of the energy sources shifts in beneficial ways. What is marked in both scenarios, however, is the reduced reliance on traditional sources of electricity ("Trad Elec"), and the rise of biomass fuels, possibly available as a byproduct of more timber cutting and the pursuit of alternative cash crops to replace tobacco. Some solar power use was included in 2025 under the Restructured Combined Change scenario. However, we limited this adaptation given the constraint imposed by the existence of a major system of electric delivery infrastructure. Obviously, major impacts on total energy use are possible for the state.

Despite these possible improvements, the decisions facing the people of the state may be far more difficult than we had previously realized. Acting in the best interests of the future will not be easy, and households, firms and policy makers face difficult choices. Households and firms will have to select between alternative available production technologies, or decide whether to invest in energy saving devices. In state policy, tradeoffs are likely to be necessary. We may have to weigh the level of effort to increase recycling against the resources to develop new means to minimize the negative environmental impacts of growth. In this context, the results of the state comparative risk assessment process become even more important. Such risk assessments may provide a basis for choosing the "lesser of two evils" when one is faced with such difficult choices. To the extent that we are able to use the comparative risk findings to set priorities between actions or desired conditions, the process of defining such risks might help us make rational and constructive choices for the good of current and future citizens of the state.

However, it is necessary to better understand the implications of the restructured economy for regional conditions and specific pollutants or environmental threats, and to review the relative roles of technological change and shifts in policies and practices for both Projections. Unless regional shifts constitute a major issue in these comparisons, we simplify the argument by examining only the state as a whole.

The range of change: Baseline status quo vs. restructured combined change

The next step is to compare the Baseline Status Quo Scenario (BSQ) to the Restructured Combined Change Scenario (RCC). This comparison sets the range of values for the scenarios considered to be the most likely. In doing so, we can consider a range of change in those values compared to the present, as we did in Figure 6.7. In this manner, we can get a sense of the extent to which the many assumptions we have made might affect future environmental conditions in the state and the problems or prospects that will remain potential problems under virtually any foreseeable future.

We begin with some more good news. Under the RCC, the more environmentally optimistic scenario we considered, the annual rate of new deposits into municipal waste disposal facilities would fall by 17 per cent, a considerable drop. Solid waste generation drops farther in the East due to population losses, and drops less in the Bluegrass due to population gains. Under the BSQ, new solid waste generated would have risen in proportion to the population; this was perhaps optimistic, as we had not included the current rising trend in per capita waste generation. However, even this very positive finding does not mean that new landfills will not continue to be needed. While the rate of new waste generated will fall, the total waste requiring disposal will continue to rise, since new waste is still generated each year.

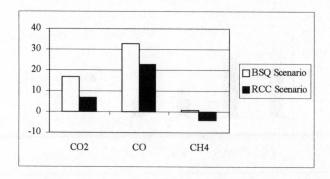

Figure 6.8   Change in greenhouse gas emissions, 1995-2025: Baseline status quo vs. restructured combined change scenarios

Emission performance results of the comparison between the BSQ and the RCC are mixed. Clearly, the RCC would result in far fewer emissions per year than the BSQ, as can be seen by the favorable comparisons for all measured emissions in Figures 6.8 and 6.9. We had already noted that the BSQ trends in emissions are probably not permissible under current law or acceptable in terms of human health. However, Figures 6.8 and 6.9 indicated worsening conditions in comparison to the present. This held under either the "environmental" or in the "no change" scenario, for the annual releases of all air pollutants other than methane (CH4), and total suspended particulates (TSP). Although the RCC showed fewer annual releases, we must remember that the elimination of a pollutant would be a 100 per cent negative percentage change. The best result we showed was a decrease of not quite five per cent under current release levels. In both scenarios, we still saw increases in greenhouse gasses released annually. This was not unexpected, since power generation and use contributes significantly to air pollution, and we saw in Figure 6.7 that total energy consumption would continue to rise under both scenarios.

One promising note, however, is the drop in the difference in the projected change in volatile organic compound (VOC) releases from the BSQ to the RCC. The drop to a 0 per cent increase for the RCC suggests that it may be attainable, provided the emissions were successfully controlled in the current non-attainment counties. Nonetheless, the conclusion to be drawn from Figures 6.8 and 6.9 is that statewide air quality is projected to get worse under all the scenarios considered in this project.

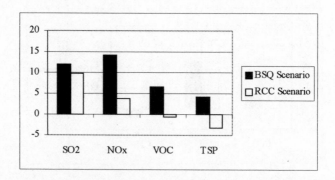

Figure 6.9   Change in ground-level emissions, 1995-2025: Baseline status quo vs. restructured combined change scenarios

The results of this comparison showed that despite allowing for currently anticipable shifts to environment preserving technologies, pro-conservation values, and regulatory practices that require these changes, environmental conditions will worsen. An exception, albeit a somewhat superficial one, was the reduction in solid waste brought about by behavioral and regulatory changes. Another bright spot came in the area of energy, where we found that usage would increase at a reduced rate, producing consequent declines in the rates of growth of greenhouse gas emissions. However, both energy usage and emissions would see continued growth.

Comparing the Baseline Status Quo scenario to the Restructured Combined Change scenario, we can derive a sense of the extent to which our assumptions about the policy context might affect future environmental

116

conditions. Under the most extreme changes explored, the rate of municipal solid waste generated could decrease substantially. Under both scenarios, annual releases of almost all air pollutants will worsen. The exceptions are that under the Restructured Combined Change, emissions of methane (CH4) and total particulates (TSP) will lessen somewhat. We will also see annual increases in greenhouse gas emissions in both scenarios. It would appear, however, that the rate of VOC releases would stay the same as at present under the Restructured Combined Change scenario. Nevertheless, the overall conclusion to be drawn is that, statewide, air quality will worsen under all the scenarios we have considered.

Implications for current policy: Sources of challenge, sources of hope

We have devoted most of our attention thus far to two of the eight different scenarios for which we constructed possible environmental futures. We began with the Baseline Status Quo Scenario (BSQ) that allowed for no changes in any aspect of the way that the level of human activity translates into environmental impacts in the state. In the BSQ, population and economic output trends generate environmental impacts, the same way they are at present. Then, we introduced the possibility of shifts in the economy generated by a combination of market and other external forces and conscious policy on the part of the state government. The Status Quo scenario under the Restructured Projection approximates this condition. However, we noted that the same forces likely to produce a restructuring of the state economy would also involve changes in household tastes and behaviors and business priorities and practices, as well as possible regulatory shifts. Thus we shifted our focus to consideration of the main alternative to the BSQ, the Restructured Combined Change Scenario (RCC).

We turn now to the partial change scenarios that lie between these extremes, looking at our output data to discover what elements make significant differences in the results. The three elements we investigated included changing technologies and their adoption, shifting regulatory practices and behaviors, or the restructuring of the economy. Given the limited fiscal capacity of any state government, there are a limited number of policies and expenditures a state can make. The state might well choose to invest in those with the highest return, in terms of overall benefit per expenditure. Will a state derive a higher return from investments in technological changes and improvements, or through investing a similar amount in stimulating attitudinal and behavioral changes and in regulatory enforcement?

117

We chose to analyze the concept of benefit, like return, through a broad-based comparison between economic structure, technological change, and policy change. To answer the question of what kind of changes or investments yield the highest benefit or return we singled out the impacts attributable to each area. In practice, the three sources of change are at least partially interconnected. However, in this analysis, we isolate them as much as possible to determine the relative strength of their contribution to an overall shift. To do this, we will compare scenarios involving the shifts presented in Tables 5.1, 5.2, and 5.3, taken one group at a time.

We begin with the forces that drive any impacts, the structure of the economy. The possibility that an economy may be significantly restructured needs to be considered in any forecast that attempts a thirty year projection. Then we turn to an examination technological change as another form of externally generated potential modifications in impacts. We conclude with a look at the changes that can be generated by conscious effort, education, policy change, and leadership, within the state. First, we will describe the effects in the forecasts, outlined in Table 5.1, that can be attributed to the Restructured Projection construction separate from other variables.

The structural economic changes that we posited in Table 5.1 included two driven by external forces in spite of state efforts. These were a major decline in tobacco farming and a drop in total coal output. Another three changes were included that would represent successful pursuit of economic development by the state, in the context of external market conditions. These included an expansion of manufacturing activity overall, with special success in secondary wood processing and accelerated private woodlot timber harvest, and further development of tourism utilizing existing cultural and ecological attractions.

Our initial comparison of the Baseline to the Restructured Projections showed that both higher GDP per person and more negative environmental impacts would occur under the Restructured Projection for the Status Quo Scenario; this was illustrated in Table 6.2. Regionally, the Restructured Projection produced more intense negative effects for the Eastern region. This reflected the probable location of new manufacturing activity in more accessible parts of the state. Additionally, we found that the higher energy intensity of the Restructured Projection would have exceptional consequences for domestic, that is, in-state, coal utilization. This kind of restructured economy could be vulnerable to any factors that might constrain the ability of the state to utilize its own coal resources.

At the statewide level, coal replaced other fossil fuels in direct use in the Restructured economy, compared to the Baseline. The move to coal was generated by the restructuring itself. This conclusion can be drawn because

118

the increased use of coal was observed under both scenarios, the Status Quo and the Combined Change, comparing the Baseline to the Restructured Projections. Under the Combined Change scenario, while the energy use totals were significantly reduced, the distribution of the sources of power remained comparable. The significant change in the Combined Change scenario was the addition of reliance on biomass fuels, largely to replace more traditional electrical power sources.

With respect to land use and municipal solid waste generation, no visible differences emerged between the two structural economic projections. We attributed this to insignificant differences in the levels of total output between the two projections. As well, incomplete data from the state government made it impossible to examine impacts on water quality, using the linkages we would have been able to model. However, basic data on the utilization of agricultural chemicals for different crops indicated one clearly beneficial environmental impact associated with restructuring. A decrease in fertilizer and other chemical applications could be expected to occur, associated with a 50 per cent decrease in acreage committed to tobacco. While it might have local significance, this decrease would be unlikely to have a high impact statewide, because the total acreage devoted to all forms of tobacco amounted to only about 1 per cent of all field cropped land.

We noted earlier that the Status Quo Scenario for the Restructured projection is highly unlikely to occur. If the economic restructuring were to take place, it would likely be accompanied by other changes in beliefs and behaviors. As well, in light of the air pollution issues we have noted, there is real doubt that the Status Quo scenario could be attained legally and politically. In any case, it does not appear that economic restructuring would reshape the relationship between economic activity and the environment in the state.

The next step in our analysis was the comparison of the effects of the two sets of possible changes, in technology and in policy. Although the two groups of actions are not unrelated to each other, we isolated and compared their impact to see which contributed the most to enhancing sustainability and reducing negative environmental impacts. The Technology Change Scenario (TCS) was developed using only that set of changes in technological performance assumptions listed in Table 5.2. Similarly, the Policy-Practice Change Scenario (PCS) was a scenario that singles out changes in policies, attitudes and behaviors, listed in Table 5.3. The TCS incorporated a string of technological changes, largely in energy efficiency and emissions controls, that appeared readily available or might be expected soon. The PCS assumed that no technological changes would occur, but that behaviors would change, such as increased recycling, the adoption of fluorescent lighting, and

119

purchases of more efficient appliances. Neither scenario, as we have noted, is truly realistic, since the policy context shifts that may be expected involve combinations of attitudinal, behavioral, and technological changes. The linkage here is obvious: changing attitudes and tastes lead both to new and different behaviors and new demands for technologies that serve the new preferences that emerge.

The relative importance of the TCS and the PCS may have major implications for state public policy efforts to minimize the negative effects of economic activity on the environment of the state. If the TCS is more important, then public efforts should be devoted to getting businesses, households and government in the state to search out and adopt the most advanced environmentally protective technologies available. Alternatively, if the PCS have the larger impact on future pollution releases and other impacts, then the government of the state should commit resources to education. These efforts could include the promotion of environmental literacy, a reexamination of environment-related regulations and policies, and the enhancement of working relationships with community groups, civic associations, churches and others to encourage behaviors that enhance sustainability.

We conducted a series of comparisons between the two scenarios, employing both the Baseline Projection and the Restructured Projection, since the two pictures of the future state economy have different impacts. Despite generally heavier environmental demands associated with the Restructured Projection, dominant patterns are clear. Both technological and policy change can significantly reduce adverse environmental impacts. Both types of change show consistently lower increases in potential or actual pollutants than does the Status Quo, and this finding holds across both projections. Policy and practice changes and other altered behaviors could serve to reduce the impacts of continued economic and population growth. However, the technological changes that are already available or are close to development promise far greater reductions in adverse environmental impacts.

Technology changes seem to hold substantially more immediate promise than do shifts in policies and practices. This was a consistent finding across impacts, with two exceptions. Changes in technology resulted in approximately 12 per cent greater reduction in total energy demand over changes in policies and practices, across both the Baseline and the Restructured projections. Technological changes resulted in larger reductions in all types of air emissions except methane. Most of these emissions reductions were on the order of 5-10 per cent greater than those resulting from policy changes, across both economic projections. For methane emissions however, changes in policy offered greater promise.

120

On the other hand, changes in policy offered by far greater promise for the reduction of solid waste, and for related reduction in methane emissions. The unrealized potential for recycling, which involves changes in policies and behaviors, offers the greatest potential for reduction in this area. A significant proportion of methane emissions seems to be linked to solid waste generation.

Results from the scenario comparison also illustrate the importance of energy policy and generation sources. Energy consumption and generation account for the majority of air pollution emissions. Since electric power generation is a large proportion of this, the fuel mix chosen for electric power generation is a significant determinant of total air emissions. In our matrix of scenarios, only the TCS allowed for the utilization of biomass as a source of electrical power, because primarily technological change was required for its implementation. This is the single most significant determinant of the better performance of the TCS over the PCS. The difference in energy sources between the scenarios and their consistency across the projections helps explain the consistency of the comparative findings.

At the level of the state, the priorities for environment-promoting efforts seem clear, other things being equal. However, we know from our earlier examination of air pollution impacts in Figures 6.1 and 6.2 that exceptional problems of rising contamination exist for two regions, the Bluegrass and Central Regions. These two regions experience the most changes and environmental threats in the projections we considered. Our conclusions about the appropriateness of the state promoting adoption of advanced technologies for environmental protection should be examined for their effects on the exceptional air pollution problems originally projected for them.

In the Central Region, new electrical power generation facilities appeared to be causing air pollution problems in the Status Quo Scenario for both projections. Under the Baseline Status Quo scenario, the Central region was projected to see sulfur dioxide emissions increase 81 per cent over current levels and nitrous oxides increase 41 per cent over current levels. The Restructured economy under the Status Quo would be slightly worse, at 112 per cent for sulfur dioxide and 56 per cent for nitrous oxides. While the PCS changes would lower these increases marginally, the effects of the changes in the TCS would be to reduce these increases approximately by half for both kinds of emissions across both projections. Emission increases are cut in half in the Central region under the TCS because total energy demand is reduced. In the TCS, total energy demand is actually reduced in the Central region. Changes in technology, and not foreseeable policy shifts, appear to have the greatest potential for reducing future demands for traditionally generated electricity. Future demand for electricity from traditional sources is cut by 50 per cent of current demand levels or more.

Similarly, technological changes have greater impact than changes in policy in the Bluegrass Region, for the pollutants of concern. In the Bluegrass, ground level emissions are a limitation on environmental quality and possibly on economic development. With technological changes, the volume of particulates emitted can actually be reduced, as increases in VOCs projected under the status quo are virtually eliminated and the rate of carbon monoxide emissions halved. Policy shifts, on the other hand, may actually make carbon monoxide emissions worse and otherwise have only marginal effects on emissions of ground level pollutants relative to the Status Quo Projection.

In consideration of the problem air quality areas in the Bluegrass region, we can predict that without technological changes with associated reductions in VOC emissions, economic growth over the next thirty years would be severely impaired. While the PCS does show improvement over the status quo, but this relative gain is not sufficient to provide assurance that conditions could be maintained or improved in the severely polluted areas of the region without further constraints on new growth and development.

In practice, it is not possible to isolate "technological changes" from "changes in policies and practices." For example, incentive programs can be used to accelerate the implementation of technology changes. Similarly, increases in recycling behaviors are to some extent technological changes, as the recycled material diverted from the solid waste stream needs to be incorporated into new products, often through new processes. The strongest finding from this evaluation is that a move to reduce emissions from electricity generation would have a large overall impact, and that the introduction of biomass fuels would have such an effect. Practically, such a move would require changes in behaviors and policies as well as the incorporation of new technologies.

Conclusions

Our starting point was the evaluation of a scenario that presumed no structural or systemic changes in the economy and its environmental linkages over the next thirty years. This scenario, the Baseline Projection and the Status Quo scenario, is both unrealistic as changes are likely to occur, and unduly pessimistic from an environmental perspective. Should things continue as they are now, the state could be facing some serious environmental problems in thirty years. The comparative analysis demonstrates that a combination of technological changes and changes in tastes, policies, and practices could improve the state's long-term environmental prospects, but even they offer no panacea.

As was the case for the Baseline Projection, the Restructured Projection involved substantial growth in the state economy, at the price of some continued deterioration of the environment. Under the Status Quo Scenario, the Restructured economy actually showed a worsening in a number of key environmental measures over the Baseline. In particular, increases would be realized in the emission of carbon dioxide (CO_2), sulfur dioxide (SO_2), and volatile organic compounds (VOCs). These increases would only exacerbate conditions in those areas in the state that are already in noncompliance with national air quality standards. It also appeared that the Restructured economy would be considerably more energy intensive than the current economy. The chief caveat regarding these findings, however, is that they assumed no technological, attitudinal, behavioral, or regulatory changes over the thirty-year period — an unrealistic assumption.

Comparing the Baseline Status Quo to the Restructured Combined Change evaluates gains that might be achieved through a generally pro-environmental shift from the present. The Restructured Combined Change incorporated all currently plausible shifts to conservation values, environment-preserving technologies, and changes in regulatory practices. Comparison to the Baseline shows much better performance in energy usage and in solid waste management, and overall lower emission levels. However, environmental conditions will worsen in comparison to the present on all measures except per capita solid waste generation and total methane and particulate emissions.

In our attempts to evaluate the relative contribution of technological changes compared to policy and practice changes, in general technological changes resulted in larger improvements in results. Alone, both sets of changes resulted in some improvement in environmental impacts relative to the Status Quo Scenario. And either one alone was inferior to both combined in reducing relative impacts. Policy changes performed better than changes in technology in impacts relative to waste volumes: solid waste generation and methane emissions. However, this finding is relative to the categorization of actions as "technological" and "policy-practice" in Tables 5.2 and 5.3. While we can isolate these changes for an analysis, they are not in practice isolated.

Our key finding was that elements of the state environment, most prominently air quality, would deteriorate over the next thirty years under either economic projection and under either scenario. This finding held even when all the changes in environmentally sensitive technologies and in policies, practices and behaviors were incorporated. Environmental factors would be likely to slow the rate of economic growth that might otherwise be expected from the economic prospects of the state. The economic future of the state is likely to be increasingly sensitive to the quality of environmental protection.

In the context of limited funds, state environmental protection efforts should be directed toward accelerating the introduction of new technologies, in particular those that reduce emissions from electricity generation, and those that reduce total energy demand. Recycling was also recommended as an effective policy for the reduction of solid waste generation. Clearly, the ideal is both technological and policy and practice change that moves in the direction of sustainable economic development. However, in the context of the budgetary constraints faced by all state governments, the current emphasis should be on facilitating key technological changes since they can have more impact than even major modifications in behaviors. Of course, the acceptance and implementation of new technologies will be facilitated with improvements in environmental literacy. In the ideal, state policies should combine the promotion of technological innovations with the promotion of environmental literacy and efforts to change wasteful behaviors. This combination offers the most promise for future environmental quality.

Note

1   The various elements of air pollution for which growth is projected in Figures 6.1 and 6.2 and throughout the chapter, are as follows:

   CO   carbon monoxide, a greenhouse gas and poison
   CO2   carbon dioxide, the primary greenhouse gas
   CH4   methane, a flammable hydrocarbon and greenhouse gas
   SO2   sulfur dioxide, noxious and poisonous gas, contributor to smog
   NOX   nitrous oxide, contributes to smog and ground level pollution
   VOC   volatile organic compounds, hydrocarbon residues, contributing to ozone buildup and smog
   TSP   total suspended particulates, the key element in smog

All of these emissions pose potential threats to ecosystems and human health as their presence increases. The discussion here dwells on the major shifts in levels of emissions, as these are the ones most likely to pose problems in the future.

7 Forecasting for sustainability conclusions, findings and potential

Our intent in this project was to move economic policy discourse in the state towards greater sustainability. Through evaluation of the likely environmental impacts of economic strategies, we sought to engage policy makers involved in the consideration of economic policy choices to include consideration of their environmental impacts. Our comparative forecasting method was directed to overcoming some existing barriers to planning for sustainability. As in most policy contexts, there is a focus on the immediate concerns of the short-term. In seeking policy relevance we needed to make our forecasts of immediate relevance and responsive to existing priorities. We consider that our research was successful in engaging its audience. In relating air quality outcomes to limitations on economic prosperity, we may have gained some ground for the acceptability of environmental concerns in this policy context.

We did encounter significant limitations in modeling and measurement for policy relevant research. While some of these barriers could be significantly reduced through better data and better linkages to environmental impacts, we consider two of these issues to be durable. The first issue is the limitations placed on the scope of change that can be considered by the requirements of plausibility for specific policy audiences. To gain an audience, the universe of plausible choices must be limited. Second, the assessment and comparison of scenarios is limited by the extent to which policy analysis can evaluate the best outcomes due to limitations on the valid measurement of values. Both of these issues, plausibility and value measurement, combine to limit the gains in policy rationality or efficiency that can be achieved through improved data availability or improved access to resources.

125

In the presentation of our methods in carrying out our forecasting project in Kentucky, we intended to provide an example of a methodological approach to policy analysis for sustainable development. In this chapter, we will briefly summarize the results of our project, and assess the reception of our project among our policy audience. We will discuss the contribution of our methodological approach in relation to the constraints of policy relevance. Rather than seeking optimal rationality or the acceptance of a far-off vision, we argue for an incremental approach grounded in immediate credibility.

First, we discuss the potential for policy analysis directed to the assessment of overall priority through a combination of environmental risk assessment and environmental impact forecasting. In addition to the limitations that are placed on research by the demands of policy relevance, there are limitations to the overall gains that are achievable through more comprehensive valuation or assessment information. There is some potential for a blend of comparative risk findings with environmental forecasts; here we draw on rudimentary links we were able to establish. There are measurement issues common to both endeavors. We then review the constraints associated with data limitations encountered in this study and the potential for joint forecasts in settings with better or more complete and detailed data. Finally, we conclude with a discussion of the potential for improved policies achievable through the comparison of alternative environmental futures.

Forecasting for sustainability

In its broad outlines, sustainable development has become a vision of a development outcome that has some acceptance among policy makers, environmentalists, academics and industry. The concept of sustainable development emphasizes a balanced relationship between ecology, economy and social life, for current and future generations. While there is wide agreement on the concept of sustainable development, there are many obstacles to the implementation of sustainable policies. Input to the policy process that seeks to affect the sustainability of future policies must address existing policy conditions.

There is more than one way to seek change. Advocates and activists seek to change public values or perception, or to promote a specific vision of a sustainable future. Some forms of sustainability research seek to improve our understanding of the social and technological requirements of a society that would ensure an equitable share of opportunities to future generations. However, sustainability research that seeks to influence the actions of current policy makers must address the requirements of policy context.

In developing information for policy, attention must be paid to crafting the information to the policy context. The policy context includes the boundaries of policy concern, the window of opportunity for input and the policy audience.

Input to the policy process should be developed with an audience of policy makers in mind. Policy is made on some middle ground of the currently accepted views held by policy makers and politicians (Fiorino 1995). While there is relatively wide acceptance of some version of sustainable development, there are significant differences in the defining conditions of sustainable development visions. These differences are akin to different views of a good life, or a good society. That is, there is no one definitive development path that would be accepted by all constituencies as constituting sustainable development.

Many advocates of sustainable development feel that the goals and the implementation of sustainable development are obvious. Among some of the policy makers that made up our relevant policy audience, we found a resistance to both planning and to environmentalism. In part, this was in response to economic concerns over a potential tradeoff between prosperity and environmental protection. As well, the policy audience represented significant established interests in current economic activities and lifestyles.

The boundaries of policy concern are usually both substantive and geographic. Substantively, policy is made in focused policy contexts. While sustainability requires a holistic approach, current policy institutions tend to have limited institutional roles, a single area focus and a limited mandate. Policy makers, however, often bound their consideration of strategies to one specific policy area. For example, economic development strategies are chosen with regard to their likely economic effects. Not only is this approach to viewing the problem likely to produce unintended effects on the environment, in the medium to longer term, these environmental effects may constrain the success of the chosen economic development strategy.

Geographically, policy is usually made with reference to the political boundaries of the policy makers, and often with reference to regional political alliances within those boundaries. In our case, the boundaries included the state as a whole and the regions of the state where interests were significantly different. For economy-environment forecasting, these boundaries are not necessarily germane to the impacts or to their measures. However, policy makers are more accustomed to using political boundaries as meaningful proxies for the measurement of economic prosperity.

Implementation of a sustainable development vision implies that choices in any one area require the assessment of consequences in other areas. An economic strategy ought to be evaluated for its environmental and social

127

performance as well as its economic performance. Assessment of these visions, and comparisons between them, require some form of acceptable measurement.

Some barriers to planning for sustainability can be seen as a product of uncertainty or a lack of information. Problems are complex, and the assessment of future consequences is uncertain. However, the lack of reliable information about the future is a permanent feature of the policy landscape. However, a lack of data is only the first dimension of the problem.

Data is constructed and analyzed through systems of measurement, or systems of valuation. Just as a lack of consensus over the procedural and substantive norms of sustainable development presents a barrier to the implementation of sustainable development policy, this same lack of consensus presents a barrier to the development of acceptable measurements. We found a lack of consensus over visions of a desirable future.

Issues of measurement and of engagement with the existing policy context are related to each other. Both are issues of credibility. In order to craft policy research that has the potential to move the policy agenda towards sustainability, the research must have sufficient credibility to warrant action. To make decisions, policy makers use information that is found to be sufficiently reliable and well founded. Judgments about the sufficiency and quality of information in public discourse can be based upon the extent to which it is in accord with prevalent political views, the character and reliability of its source just as much as more technical judgments of methodological quality. These incremental decisions about economic strategy, social policy and ecological health are made in existing policy contexts. The policies chosen in the existing policy contexts, whether based on explicit concern for some view of sustainability or not, together constitute a policy direction.

Forecasting Kentucky's environmental futures: A summary

In our analysis of the longer-term prospects for the state of Kentucky, we found that environmental quality was likely to deteriorate over time under all the scenarios that we examined. The incorporation of significant behavioral changes and technological changes would lessen the rate of deterioration. However, under the impact linkage models we used, all scenarios involved environmental quality growing worse than at present. Drawing on both political and economic factors, we concluded that this deterioration was likely to retard future economic expansion along any of the paths considered plausible.

128

The scenarios had been constructed to respond to the concerns of policy makers. We used input from policy makers and from policy processes to develop plausible scenarios, and to establish plausible ranges of behavioral changes. The economic sectors that formed the focus of our scenario building efforts were those identified by policy makers as priority sectors for the state. The scope of the scenarios was actually quite limited by these conceptions of the plausible or possible in the state. The range of changes considered for the coal industry and the tobacco industry were quite limited. These were the two traditional resource sectors at risk in a future, more sustainable economy.

At the conclusion of the first stage of the project, we had an initial list of priorities for our work. We had a working description of the current state of the economy and a sense of what the first priority environmental problems were in the state. We also had an idea of what the difference in opinion and perception was between policy makers' and environmental researchers' as to priority issues for policy action on environmental issues. While we continued to gather data from many sources and to evaluate approaches to environmental impact forecasting, we began the next step in our project: setting up an advisory group of policy makers we would involve in further work and in a social learning process.

Once we had the model assembled, and had constructed some scenarios and projections for testing, we were able to assess the longer-term implications of current economic policy choices for certain environmental variables. Our scenario reasoning, preliminary results and further testing are detailed in Chapters Five and Six. Once we began to run the model and derive some initial results, we found that within the constraints considered reasonable, no economic development path accepted as plausible be environmentally viable according to current environmental performance standards. This finding is instructive, and enlightening in itself. Without positing any conditions that were not believable or trusted, our model showed serious problems under any normal conditions. It was our hope that this finding would assist those who argued for environmental policies and education not currently considered feasible. Our response was to test our model for the policy combinations with the greatest impact across a set of economic projections.

Our report also recommended that policies that promoted environmental literacy were important to the environmental future of the state. This was a policy priority developed in the course of the advisory group process. As well, increases in environmental literacy might increase the scope of the behavioral and value changes necessary to avoid some of the impacts found likely in our modeling effort.

129

Our analytical efforts in this project were incomplete, as a forecast of environmental impacts. However, the project should be considered a qualified success. Due to the time constraints and the limitations of the data that was available to us, our analysis was limited primarily to air quality effects. We could not model other environmental impacts of priority interest to policy makers, such as water quality. However, our study illustrated the potential that such analyses may prove to be useful bases for improved decision-making.

With greater resources and data on environmental impacts as well as more in depth study of individual and small group preferences, there is potential for such studies to provide a much more complete picture of the environmental consequences of different economic strategies. As concern over environmental quality grows, the data available for the identification of the environmental consequences of economic and regulatory or policy alternatives will improve. Similarly, with increasing attention to the broader effects of alternative futures, the resources for improving the information on which choices can be made will grow.

Environmental research for the policy process: Context and credibility

One goal of our project was to move the policy dialogue in the direction of greater sustainability, while remaining responsive to current constraints. One contribution of our method that can be translated and applied in other contexts, is that research that seeks to affect implementation must engage an existing audience and an existing policy context. The centrality of our advisory group process to adapting the research project to the existing policy audience illustrates one way to design policy relevance into sustainability research. We chose the advisory group process and applied the nominal group technique to ensure that our forecast would respond to policy priorities and remain within the limits of plausibility. These elements are central to establishing credibility with a policy audience.

The context of our project was typical of policy contexts. We had to respond to many constraints on our resources and limitations to the possibility of comprehensiveness. Constraints on time and data availability are typical in policy contexts, as are constraints on the form and content of input. We also attempted to ensure that our forecasting engaged previous and concurrent projects relevant to our policy audience and to our project by using existing policy documents. While a policy context provides constraints, it also provides a window of opportunity for relevant input. We met the time and resource constraints of this policy-making window.

In assessing our success, we considered several measures. Since this was input into a broad policy process, it is difficult to attribute impact or influence in terms of changes or implementations made. However, we can approximate some measure of immediate response. As well, we can assess our success in engaging our policy audience. As a longer-term impact, we also propose that our project did assist in moving the policy discourse in a more sustainable direction.

In measuring the immediate influence of our report, we turn first to measures of its distribution within the state. The demand for copies of the report was over twice as high as we had expected. Initially, we had estimated a demand for about 1200 copies, with 900 of these delivered to parties within the state of Kentucky. About 200 of these were delivered to federal policy makers, primarily in Washington. We kept 100 copies for our own distribution network.

Following the initial distribution, the state had at least another 1000 copies produced and distributed. At the federal level, an additional 100 copies were required. As well, we produced approximately another 400 copies ourselves to handle direct requests. In all, we estimated that approximately 2700 paper copies of the report were distributed. As well, the document has since been made available on compact disc by the state, but since it is packaged with other policy documents we cannot estimate how many copies of our report were requested. Abbreviated versions of the report were also published in a policy collection, and released in a periodical directed to policy makers (Lyons, Meyer and Mani 1996; LTPRC 1996).

Articles in state newspapers served to further distribute the results of the report; some of these represented the results accurately and well (e.g. Melnykovych 1996). Other, more editorial, articles allowed us to judge initial response to our report, and to look for the message that had been heard. Most of the articles headlined the conclusion that declines in environmental quality could hurt the economy of the state. Three editorials focussed on the economy-environment link, using our report as further evidence to buttress the argument that good environmental controls make good business sense (n.a. 1996a; n.a. 1996b; n.a. 1996c). Another, putting less emphasis on business, advised that people in the state needed to make changes in their behaviors to avoid environmental degradation (Mead 1996).

Only one article was written in a clearly skeptical way, including opinions of those who felt that the report had overstated the case. This was written from the Central region where air quality had been projected to decline from the increased use of coal. Those quoted cited examples of technological and behavioral changes that could be made (Minor 1996). However, the changes they mentioned had already been accounted for and incorporated in our

131

project. On the one hand, it was clear that neither the author nor those quoted had read the report or a summary version. On the other hand, it is likely that the Central region policy audience, including industrial and commercial interests in the expected coal-fueled energy production, were not attracted to a report that predicted large changes in air quality in that region as a result of that new production. It is likely that these regional predictions were larger and more negative than some parts of our state audience were prepared to contemplate.

Our findings about air quality and economic development, in particular, were unexpected. While the basic interrelationship between a healthy economy and a healthy environment was not new to some, our impression was that the specific results were shocking to people. However, since the report was based on assumptions that were uncontroversial, the findings overall were judged to be reliable, and its conclusions were taken seriously for the most part. Our report was set in the context of familiar regions and familiar industries, the industries of greatest concern in the state. The predictions were grounded, in sources considered authoritative in the state. As well, the scenarios were constructed without leaps in cultural or political assumptions that, while possible, are unlikely to be believable to policy makers. Overall, we produced justifiable predictions, about issues of concern to policy makers, using their input.

The effect on policy or program implementation of a single report is difficult to measure. No formal legislation was passed in direct response to our report, but the report has influenced the debate on environmental policy in the state. The policy implications of our report were in many ways difficult to implement, and difficult to interpret simply. For one thing, no one path emerged as promising improvement in environmental conditions, so there was no clear positive recommendation. This is an important finding, although it is not a particularly palatable one from a political perspective. This finding may eventually serve to generate demand for alternative policies and new choices, but it generates no immediate solutions. The policy issues that emerged were thorny, such as the role of the car in air quality. A large proportion of the air quality problems that we projected in urban areas stemmed from the use of the car.

It is possible that had we been able to obtain data on water quality, we might have discovered that the different projections and scenarios considered included at least one in which the conditions in that environmental medium could have been improved. Such an outcome would have been preferable, since the process of selection across least damaging alternatives is politically unappealing.

However, we believe that our report was part of a set of policy documents that did affect policy making in Kentucky, in the formation of its environmental education strategy. The state of Kentucky has developed a strong and proactive approach to the improvement of environmental literacy and environmental education. While Kentucky lags behind in many areas of environmental policy, it is a leader in environmental education. For example, over the last four years, most states have taken legislative action in common and significant areas of environmental policy such as waste treatment, brownfields legislation and state mandates for local land use planning. While other states forge ahead, the state of Kentucky lags behind, with no significant policy movement in any of these areas. In this comparative context, Kentucky's innovative environmental education strategy is a notable exception. In the time period since the release of our report, Kentucky has spent a total of $2 million on environmental education directed to both children and adults.

Although Kentucky lags in most areas of environmental policy, it is a leader in environmental education. In our report, environmental education was identified as the highest priority policy area and as vital to the future environmental health of the state. In the state comparative risk assessment, environmental education was identified as one of forty action strategies; included in these forty were at least four other action priorities that involved changes in the environmental awareness of citizens of the state (NREPC 1997). And, environmental awareness had been identified as one of twenty-five long term goals in an ongoing strategic planning and visioning process undertaken by the Long Term Policy Research Center (LTPRC 1996). Our report was one of a number of reports that identified environmental literacy, education or awareness as a vital and important factor in state policy. Together, these reports probably did have an effect on the degree to which the state has invested in environmental education.

Although we constrained our assumptions to meet our audience's expectations and beliefs about realities in the state, we still produced a report that recommended serious changes in environmental performance over time. Even if current beliefs about plausible alternatives are accepted as model drivers, it may well be possible to derive sturdy conclusions for policy, or to illustrate the need to look further. Such research can support the development of new options and broaden the public's understanding of the choices available.

There is a tension between the plausibility and acceptability of research and the extent to which it can be comprehensive. In limiting our scenarios to those considered plausible by the state policy audience, we had to limit the range of possible change we could consider in accordance with a set of more or less established beliefs. This problem is likely to occur in other settings. There are likely to be divergent perspectives on the plausibility of pursuit of different alternatives. This problem is common to both purely economic and economy-environment forecasting. In a purely economic decision context, development paths that anticipate the decline of dominant employment or income-generating sectors may never be considered, in part because their non-economic costs may never have been identified. The need to even contemplate alternative economic activities may go unrecognized — or those other sectors may provide lower monetary returns and thus be bypassed because of "obvious inferiority." Over time, perhaps because of a degree of institutional path dependence, different economic bases and activities may come to be considered implausible. Dominant industries and even technologies tend to get institutionalized politically as well as economically, so paths to economic development that diverge from past patterns may never be considered.

In projects that attempt to assess the combination of economic and environmental impacts, the decision-problem becomes more complex. Choices based on the dual consideration of environmental and economic impacts, however, may define some neglected paths as appropriate and defensible, given a broader decision context and new criteria. This possibility must be created either through engaged research, through environmental education, or through other attempts to broaden the development discourse such as advocacy. Practically, some options desirable from some perspectives may be difficult or impossible to include in a given policy context, due to concerns with the policy audience as a whole.

The emergence of the service economy in the United States in the latter decades of the twentieth century provides one object example of this problem. The decline in manufacturing employment was decried, the maintenance of median incomes in a shift to services employment rejected as even remotely possible, and the trends resisted by local, state and national economic policies. A services path to wealth and income expansion was rejected as implausible, as much because of institutionalized commitments to past patterns of development as because of uncertainty over the outcomes of the emerging alternative. Unions, in collusion with major manufacturing firms, resisted the shift in order to protect their own workers and stockholders, and both had sufficient political power to generate the public resistance to the change that was evident in the 1970s and 1980s. Policies to support acceleration of the sectoral shift garnered no strong political support, even though such interventions might have had the effect of making the changes less onerous for workers and investors who experienced economic losses in the transition. The experience of the 1990s demonstrates that the

134

path could, and did, produce great wealth, continued economic expansion, and an increase in mean and median incomes, albeit at the cost of increases in income inequality in the country that might have been avoided.

On the one hand, for policy relevant research it is necessary to limit scenarios to alternatives considered to be real or plausible. And yet, we have experience with changes that were not considered to be real or plausible as they were occurring. Accordingly, there is a need for engaged research that presses at the boundaries of plausibility about the future while retaining sufficient credibility to be considered in policy. Depending on the intent of the research, careful attention should be paid to considerations of an audience appropriate to a purpose.

Some sustainability research seeks to engage an audience in the formation of visions of sustainability in order to engender thinking about new kinds of possibilities and to broaden the imagination of goals. For example, a set of scenarios can be constructed that describe broadly different futures dependent on different sets of values and changes. Costanza (2000) provides an example of this kind of sustainability research. Four scenarios are presented, and readers of the online journal Conservation Ecology are invited to vote on preferable scenarios (Costanza 2000). This kind of research might be valuable in defining preferable visions of the future. However, in this case the audience engaged is likely to be limited to environmentalists, both through the media of presentation and through the form and content of the scenarios.

The four scenarios presented are well characterized by their names: Star Trek, Big Brother, Mad Max and Ecotopia. The four scenarios are defined on a two dimensional matrix. One dimension is the degree of technological optimism about the future, and the other dimension is the possible outcome, good or bad. Star Trek, for example, is the future supposedly envisioned by technological optimists that see every problem solved by technological advances. Mad Max is the "downside" of Star Trek, if not all problems can be solved through technology. In Big Brother, we are controlled through a combination of technology and government. In Ecotopia, neither technology nor bureaucracy have controlling roles in problem solving; we all live in small and largely self-sufficient democratic and civil communities (Costanza 2000). Unfortunately, since it seems obvious that Ecotopia is the vision of the future that one is supposed to find desirable, the question of which vision is actually preferred seems less than straightforward. This represents a vision-oriented type of scenario research.

Vision-oriented scenario research provides a valuable contrast to our project. In both our research and more vision-oriented scenario research, there is an attempt to describe futures to inform current action. While our intention was to inform current policy, vision-oriented scenario research is intended to inform current personal choices. There is a significant contrast between the scenarios we developed and those that were developed in the example of vision-oriented research; this contrast highlights the connection between judgments of plausibility and the nature of the audience that could be engaged. The visioning scenarios are likely to be seen as implausible and therefore irrelevant to a broad spectrum of current policy audiences. Our scenarios were circumspect in their attention to the plausibility of scenarios for a specific policy audience in a specific policy context. To engage policy makers in current changes, it is necessary to limit the range of scenarios to alternatives that are judged to be real, viable, and plausible.

Given the current policy context in Kentucky, our study did not include scenarios such as reductions in the reliance on coal mining or drastic reductions in tobacco farming, two traditionally dominant sectors in the state economy. The scope of changes that might be considered plausible by another audience was not given full consideration. The options examined were chosen to assure their acceptance as political, economically and institutionally plausible. This constraint limited the scope of the paths examined — and may have precluded assessment of analytically superior choices — but was accepted in order to raise the probability that policy makers would give serious attention to the issue of choosing development paths using a dual environment and economy criterion.

To create the conditions for incremental changes in current policy, it is important to incorporate considerations of audience, scope of authority and the policy process. The audience we created for our research was as large as it was due to our attention to the immediate concerns and the mindset of current policy makers. The set of futures that are likely to be given serious consideration in a specific policy context is limited. To develop credibility, policy research must respond to these limitations.

However, these limitations limit the universe of futures that can be considered and limit the extent to which any policy relevant research can seek to be comprehensive. Accordingly, there are limitations on the substantive conclusions of policy relevant research. There can be no assurance that the optimal futures have been considered, nor that dimensions such as optimal distribution or optimal environmental quality will be entertained as credible. Accordingly, the extent to which policy relevant research can reasonably seek to be overarchingly comprehensive or rational among all options is limited. Forecasting for use in policy must respond to a limited set of futures and evaluate them from an accepted valuation perspective. Credibility for policy is also an issue of valuation, or measurement.

Issues in measurement and valuation

There are limitations to the comprehensive assessment of commensurable valuations for rational and efficient policy. These limits derive from limits on our ability to value alternatives collectively or over time. Valuation and measurement depend on shared perspectives and purposes. If the people of a state actually held values that were homogenous, or had only a small variation across a population, reasonably reliable and equitable preference functions could be developed. Even in a homogenous population in an area with little geographic variation, preferences, and therefore valuations, change over time. The limitation is to comprehensiveness, similar to the limitation on plausible scenarios. The set of scenarios that will be judged plausible for policy is smaller than the set of all possible scenarios. Similarly, the range of values that can be aggregated into a collective valuation system is limited to a smaller range of values than those that reflect the values of all constituents.

The resources that ought to be committed to determining quantitative valuations to environmental and economic strategy choice are also limited. Such determinations are complex if they are possible. Changes in the situation occur, as do changes in the way risks and outcomes are valued by people. By the time a comprehensive valuation assessment across a population was completed, it might be out of date. Over time, these changes would be sufficient to affect the valuation outcome of comparisons between strategies. At any single point in time, a collective valuation using one political boundary is likely to differ from collective valuations made at regional or small-area boundaries.

While improvements in data availability and environmental modeling can improve our ability to understand the consequences of our actions, comprehensive value assessments will not necessarily lead to improved comparisons of value, nor more rational and efficient decision-making. Long term forecasts are valuable as inputs to current policy and decision processes rather than as predictions of the future or as replacements of the policy decision process.

The Kentucky forecasting project was intended to inform the choice of an appropriate mix of strategies in the pursuit of economic development and promotion of environmental protection. Our central analytical purpose was the systematic evaluation of policy alternatives against possible future scenarios. To do this, we compared the extent to which future economic scenarios affected certain indicators of environmental quality.

Our project was expected to link the examination of alternative environmental futures to the state's comparative risk determination efforts. The goal of a combination of a comparative risk analysis and an

137

environmental futures projection is to provide the information needed for a rational, deliberative, empirically based process of decision-making. This combination would provide a systematic comparison of the environmental policy efficiency gains to be realized from improved understandings of environmental and economic processes on the part of the public.

In principle, it would be possible to combine comparative risk findings with environmental forecasts to select preferred paths for economic development. A full comparative risk assessment would allow for the valuation and comparison of outcomes across risks. Such a comparative risk assessment would use some form of voting or summation process to determine current weighted risk valuations, in a manner similar to that used to determine preferred economic outcomes. Using this information, we could determine empirically whether an outcome that improved ground water quality but resulted in increases in ground level ozone was preferable to one that was likely to lead to improved protection of surface water and biodiversity, but increases in carbon dioxide emissions.

In practice, the ability to calculate these total preference valuations would require full risk assessment ratings and comparative risk weights for all environmental risk areas and complete environmental condition forecasts for alternative futures covering the same dimensions of environmental risk. Neither the state comparative risk project nor our project were able to produce complete results. To an extent, this outcome can be attributed to constraints on the resources available to both projects; constraints that included time, financial resources and information.

Data limitations narrowed the scope of the scenarios that our project could consider. The data that were available for water quality and for economic activities affecting water quality were insufficient. Since we could not predict the impact of different alternative futures on water quality, we had inadequate information to develop water quality impact forecasts. Therefore we could not apply the relative risk rankings using the state comparative risk study. Variables of land quality posed a similar problem.

Theoretically, impacts on biodiversity could also be derived from cumulative outputs from economic activity that could be linked to habitat and toxicity impacts and then linked to species and ecological communities of concern. Here too the data that we could produce were limited to the rates of emissions and releases, but these could not be linked reliably to ecological regions. Geographically, the data on emissions are bounded according to political subdivisions. However, pollutants accumulate in, or are dispersed across, geomorphological areas, watersheds and air basins, and different areas have different ecologies and biota. Since the geography of ecosystems and that of economic systems do not correspond, these very geographically specific impacts could not be measured.

Some of these limitations can be overcome through longer-term efforts. The experience gained from these two studies should have led the state to invest the analyses that would contribute toward economic expansion with higher environmental quality. However, further efforts to quantify fully comparative risk valuations, or to develop the ability to quantitatively compare environmental outcomes are not ever likely to result in fully rational or efficient decision making as the ideal suggests.

The data that are available reflect measurements in accordance with existing systems of valuation that may or may not be relevant for environmental impact assessment. Improved data availability for environmental impact analysis could be attained through the development of data structures more appropriate for environmental analysis at the state level. This would have the potential to improve our ability to forecast a greater variety of environmental impacts with greater regional validity. However, in order to be able to compare alternative outcomes quantitatively, measurements of comparative valuation would have to be developed.

In both environmental forecasting and comparative risk assessment, the issue of valuation lies at the core of the problem. The comparative risk assessment process provides an object example of the difficulty in developing approaches to valuation that establish comparable and commensurable measurements of environmental risk for the state as a whole across all areas of environmental risk. The state comparative risk process did not arrive at common and aggregable risk measures for the different risks and exposures that were examined (NREPC 1997).

For most impact areas, scientists on the technical committees developed measurements of risk, but these were not developed into assessments of risk values. The risk measurements used had greater objectivity and "scientific validity" than combined scales could have claimed, but they were of little use in decision-making. Subjective judgments by committee-members voting on the extent of risks produced the final rankings. The inability to rate policy priorities or provide a final ranking of policy areas is not surprising. Rather, it is a typical result of environmental risk assessments. For example, it is a common finding that people are more willing to accept a given degree of risk that is voluntary than the same degree of risk that is involuntary. There are other qualities of risk, besides the assessments of physical hazard, that affect its comparative valuation.

Individual valuations will change over time, and the variability between valuations is high. This variability was evident in our advisory group process and in the public meeting records from the comparative risk assessment process (NREPC 1996). In addition to high variability between individuals, there are large variations in outcomes between regions. As well, there are likely to be changes in valuation over time. Preference functions, conclusions and priorities will vary over time and between groups. There is likely to be a point of diminishing return to quantitative comparative valuation efforts due to the relatively constant limitations on comprehensiveness and commensurability.

The comparative valuation problem is actually similar in choices between economic strategies. No two paths produce the same economic outcomes. Outcomes will differ in the distribution of benefits across people, places and sectors even if the aggregate expansion is identical. Absent any environmental impact measures, a choice of paths would be made on the basis of preferred distributional outcomes. While economics seems to have the problem of commensurable valuation solved, in fact the desirability of outcomes depends on perspectives and on the boundaries of concern. Such preferences are expressed in political processes, so the roles of ideology, regional interests, and values clearly play a central role in decisions.

For example, the risks associated with different economic and environmental changes and their comparative weights will vary across the regions of Kentucky. We have seen how air quality issues may adversely affect economic development in the Bluegrass Region. As well, population loss might have negative effects on both quality of life and physical environmental conditions in the Eastern Region. The regional analysis of outcomes enables us to differentiate between impacts. Better regionally disaggregated data would improve our ability to forecast impacts for a fuller set of environmental conditions. However, the most highly valued options would likely differ between regions due to differences in conditions, economic outcomes and the distribution of impacts.

In the comparative risk analysis, the regions for which impacts need to be considered vary significantly across the three major categories of risk. Ecological impacts are felt within geomorphological areas (watersheds, airsheds, land masses), while human health impacts may be related to economic zones and population settlement patterns, and quality of life effects include issues of population mobility, lifestyle regions, and the maintenance of diversity in different socio-political regions of the Commonwealth.

The appropriate scale at which to conduct such forecasts and comparative risk assessments is difficult to determine. Some ecological impacts and other outcomes may be seen only across wide regions. Water pollution impacts are generally shared across watersheds or river systems, although the intensity of impacts can vary with locality. Air pollution can involve massive migration of pollution, potentially skipping over hundred of miles or kilometers and descending only at a significant distance from the pollutant generators. At the same time, risk perception can be very site-specific, so efforts to assign values to intensity of environmental risk exposures may have to be focused on narrow geographic areas. Since the risks are frequently unevenly distributed even within small areas, and valuation of risk avoidance may vary with level of exposure, aggregation of local risk perceptions to some larger regional aggregate will tend to lose track of those settings placing a very high value on risk reduction efforts. Regional analysis and valuation might reflect differing concerns over the distribution across space of different levels of economic well being and quality of life. Localized ecological and human health impacts might be overlooked at the aggregate state level.

Because the variation between economic and environmental outcomes is so high between regions in Kentucky, total statewide assessments may be differ significantly from regional assessments. Different patterns of interaction between economic expansion and environmental impacts reflect spatially diverse mixes of types of economic activity. The risks assigned to the interactions, and the value placed on avoiding or reducing the likelihood of perceived negative outcomes will similarly vary. Such differences underscore the importance of public perception and public concern as the basis for action and intervention.

The wide divergence of impacts we have noted across the four regions of Kentucky underscores the role of uneven prosperity in the economy-environment decision frame. As a measure of public environmental concern, an economic logic would rely on measures of "willingness to pay" to avoid them. The form of the payment may be acceptance of environmental deterioration of some sort in one case, or reduced monetary returns in another. Each is presumed to reflect a population's understanding of the choices it faces and its selection of a preferred alternative.

This approach has value as a reflection of the options available to a population. At the same time, it is useless in conceptualizing alternatives that would be preferable if they were recognized or created. These alternatives might not be evident to a population forced into a set of choices at a given point in time. The "willingness to pay" approach also fails to address any possible unequal distribution of risks within the population exercising the choices or differences in individuals' valuations of the relative risks. Finally, since the two means of payment are either adverse environmental impacts or monetary losses, the logic accepts as appropriate the decision constraints imposed by low "ability to pay" in monetary terms. Low prosperity appears to indicate the willing acceptance of environmental deterioration.

Our project and the comparative risk assessment both gave priority to recommendations that would change the decision context and change societal

141

valuations (NREPC 1997). In both projects, environmental education was accorded a pivotal role in value change and value formation. Environmental education could help avoid a development-environment conflict through improved public understandings and would help to build political support for appropriate regulations. Both projects identified the potential for environmental regulations and enforcement efforts to shape both the directions of economic development and changes in environmental conditions; in this sense, legislation can lead preference. Together, environmental education and a growing role for positive environmental regulation in the state might assist in building a constituency for the pursuit of sustainable economic development. Together, these interrelated elements of the political and social environment were seen as holding the key to moving the state as a whole in the direction of sustainability.

It is in this context that good science and widely accessible and systematically delivered education about environmental and economic conditions and choices becomes a necessity for effective and equitable public sector action. Environmental education in its broadest forms is not a luxury, nor a frill that might be dropped by a fiscally strained education system. It is essential to accelerating the adoption of environmentally sensitive technologies that can promote more sustainable economic development. Environmental education provides the foundation for more sustainable public decisions.

Prospects: The potential contribution of environmental forecasts

As sustainable development has become more central to political agendas, the demand for analyses of sustainability have grown. As sustainability is measured over time, forecasting is a central part of the assessment of sustainability. Whether or not the pursuit of sustainable development paths is merely political rhetoric or a real effort to modify the adverse impacts of human population growth and increased economic activity on the environment, some consistent and conceptually plausible means of projecting the ecological and other results is needed.

Forecasts that permit alternatives to be compared could improve decisions regardless of the priority given to environmental considerations. Other things, being equal, healthier natural systems may be expected to contribute to a higher human quality of life. Thus, if two different paths toward the same level of economic expansion are available, and one of them can be determined will avoid the negative environmental consequences associated with its alternative, the path producing higher overall well-being can be identified and pursued.

Kentucky's first steps down the road toward assessment of economic development options in terms of the environmental, as well as economic, risks and opportunities they may present provides some indications of the potential that might be realized. A more complete analysis and integration of the two elements, comparative risk and environmental futures, holds promise for increasing the capacity of policy makers to assess the future sustainability of current policy choices.

Analytical comparisons of alternatives should be produced as inputs to the policy process, with attention to the demands of policy relevance such as credibility and timeliness. While better data are required to better estimate the environmental impacts of different strategies, the forecast and the valuation should not seek to replace the political process. Sufficient reliability in the use of data and in the presentation of options should suffice. It is unlikely that comparative analysis of environmental futures or of environmental risk will generate prescriptive results, due to the significant limitations on the development of comparative valuations. However, indicative findings can be generated that can be of value to policy debates. Fundamentally, it is not clear that the best political decision is the one that most closely corresponds to the summation of existing preferences and values. There is an important role for leadership in policy decisions and in the incremental implementation of greater sustainability.

The type of forecasting we envision is engaged research that seeks to change attitudes and understanding at the same time as it is responsive to current audiences. This approach is consistent with our recommendations about the importance of environmental education. Engaged environmental research can be an aspect of environmental education, with the potential for reshaping perceptions and preferences. In order to change current policy in the direction of more sustainable development, it is necessary to reach and engage existing policy audiences through relevant and credible research.

Bibliography

Aberley, D. (ed.), (1994), *Futures by Design: The Practice of Ecological Planning*, New Society Publishers: Philadelphia.

Arinze, B. (1994), 'Selecting Appropriate Forecasting Models Using Rule Induction', *Omega*, Vol. 22, No. 6, pp. 647-59.

Armstrong-Cummings, K., Barber, A. and Stutsman, P. (1994), *Bringing it Home: Sustainable Practices in Kentucky*, Cabinet for Natural Resources and Environmental Protection: Frankfort.

Bartelmus, P. (1994), *Environment, Growth, and Development: The Concepts and Strategies of Sustainability*, Routledge: New York.

Becker, H.A. and van Doorn, J.W.M. (1987), 'Scenarios in an Organizational Perspective', *Futures*, Vol. 19, No. 6, pp. 669-78.

Benedick, R.E. (1991), *Ozone Diplomacy*, Harvard University Press: Cambridge.

Bryson, J.M. and Roering, W.D. (1988), 'Applying Private Sector Planning in the Public Sector', in Bryson, J.M. and Einsweiler, R.C. (eds), *Strategic Planning: Threats and Opportunities for Planners*, American Planning Association: Chicago, IL.

Büscher, M. (1994), *Lessons from the Ecological Age: Values in Economics and Socio-Economic Reform of the Market Economy*, paper presented at the Sixth Annual Conference of the Society for the Advancement of Socio-Economics, Paris, France, July.

Carlin, A. (1990), *Environmental Investments: The Cost of a Clean Environment*, U. S. Environmental Protection Agency Publication EPA-230-90-084, U.S. Government Printing Office, Washington DC.

Charpin, J.M. (1986), 'Quantitative Macroeconomic Projections', *Futures*, Vol. 18, No. 2, pp. 158-70.

Childress, M.T., Schirmer, P. and Smith-Mello, M. (eds), (1999), *The Leadership Challenge Ahead: Trends That Will Dominate the Future Agenda*, Kentucky Long Term Policy Research Center: Frankfort, KY.

Childress, M.T., Sebastian, B.M., Schirmer, P. and Smith-Mello, M. (eds), (1996), *Exploring the Frontier of the Future: How Kentucky Will Live, Learn and Work*, Kentucky Long Term Policy Research Center: Frankfort, KY.

Cole, L. (1996), 'Kentucky's Environmental Trends: Progress and Problems', in Childress, M.T. *et al.* (eds), (1996), *Exploring the Frontier of the Future: How Kentucky Will Live, Learn and Work*, Kentucky Long Term Policy Research Center: Frankfort, KY.

Common, M. (1995), *Sustainability and Policy*, Cambridge University Press: Cambridge, UK.

Costanza, R. (2000), 'Visions of Alternative (Unpredictable) Futures and Their Use in Policy Analysis', *Conservation Ecology*, Vol. 4, No. 1, pp. 5 [http://www.consecol.org/vol4/iss1/art5].

Dalkey, N.C. (1967), *Delphi*, Rand Corporation: Santa Monica.

Daly, H.E. and Cobb, J.B., Jr. (1989), *For The Common Good: Redirecting the Economy Toward Community, the Environment and Sustainable Future*, Beacon Press: Boston.

Delbecq, A.L. and van de Ven, A.H. (1971), 'A Group Process Model for Problem Identification and Program Planning', *Journal of Applied Behavior Science*, Vol. 7, No. 4, pp. 467-92.

Duchin, F. and Lange, G-M. (1994), *The Future of the Environment: Ecological Economics and Technological Change*, Oxford University Press: New York.

Dutch Committee for Long-Term Environmental Policy (1994), *The Environment; Toward a Sustainable Future*, Kluwer Academic Publishers: Dordrecht.

Easterbrook, G. (1997), 'Greenhouse Common Sense: Why Global-Warning Economics Matters more than Science', *U.S. News and World Report*, December 1, pp. 58-62.

Fiorino, D. (1995), *Making Environmental Policy*, University of California Press: Berkeley, CA.

Fisher, W. (1989), *Human Communication as Narration: Toward a Philosophy of Reason, Value, and Action*, University of South Carolina Press: Columbia.

Flinn, J.E. and Reimers, R.S. (1974), *Development of Predictions of Future Pollution Problems*, Project Final Report prepared by Battelle Columbus Laboratories for the Office of Research and Development, U.S.

Environmental Protection Agency, U.S. Government Printing Office: Washington DC.

Forrester, J.W. (1971), *World Dynamics*, Wright-Allen: Cambridge, MA.

Fox, W.M. (1989), 'The Improved Nominal Group Technique', *Journal of Management Development*, Vol. 8, No. 1, pp. 20-26.

Glantz, M.H. (1991), 'The Use of Analogies in Forecasting Ecological and Societal Responses to Global Warming', *Environment*, Vol. 33, No. 5, pp. 10-23.

Goetz, S. and Schirmer, P. (1996), 'Industry Trends: Jobs and Earnings', in Childress *et al.* (eds), *Exploring the Frontier of the Future: How Kentucky Will Live, Learn and Work*, Kentucky Long Term Policy Research Center: Frankfort, KY.

Goodstein, E.B. (1994), *Jobs and the Environment: The Myth of a National Trade-Off*, Economic Policy Institute: Washington DC.

Greer, M.R. (1995), 'Aggressive Greenhouse Gas Policies: How They Could Spur Economic Growth', *Journal of Economic Issues*, Vol. XXIX, No. 4, pp. 1045-62.

Gustafson, D. H., Shukla, R. K., Delbecq, A. L. and Walster, G. W. (1973), 'A Comparative Study of Differences in Subjective Likelihood Estimates Made by Individuals, Interacting Groups, Delphi Groups and Nominal Groups', *Organ of Behavior and Human Decision Process*, Vol. 9, No. 2, pp. 280-91.

Hall, B. (1994), *Gold and Green: Can We Have Good Jobs and a Healthy Environment?*, Institute for Southern Studies: Edurham, NC.

Hendry, D.F. (1995), 'Econometrics and Business Cycle Empirics', *Journal of the Royal Economic Society*, Vol. 105, No. 433, pp. 1622-37.

Hirschhorn, J.S. and Oldenburg, K.U. (1991), *Prosperity Without Pollution*, Van Nostrand Reinhold: New York.

Hufschmidt, M.M., James, D.E., Meister, Bower, B.T. and Dixon, J.A. (1983), *Environment, Natural Systems and Development: An Economic Valuation Guide*, The Johns Hopkins University Press: Baltimore, MD.

Huggett, R.J. (1993), *Modelling the Human Impact on Nature: Systems Analysis of Environmental Problems*, Oxford University Press: Oxford, UK.

Hughes, B.B. (1999), 'The International Futures (IFs) Modeling Project', *Simulation and Gaming*, Vol. 30, No. 3, pp. 304-26.

Isard, W. (1972), *Ecologic-Economic Analysis for Regional Development*, The Free Press: New York.

Jansson, A., Hammer, M., Folke, C. and Costanza, R. (eds), (1994), *Investing in Natural Capital: The Ecological Economics Approach to Sustainability*, Island Press: Washington DC.

146

Jones, J. and Hunter, D. (1995), 'Consensus Methods for Medical and Health Research', *British Medical Journal*, Vol. 311, No. 7001, pp. 376-81.

Kaplan, T.J. (1993), 'Reading Policy Narratives: Beginnings, Middles and Ends', in Fischer, F. and Forester, J. (eds), *The Argumentative Turn in Policy Analysis and Planning*, Duke University Press: Durham, NC.

Kay, J.J., Regier, H.A., Boyle, M. and Francis, G. (1999), 'An Ecosystem Approach for Sustainability: Addressing the Challenge of Complexity', *Futures*, Vol. 31, No. 7, pp. 721-42.

Kentucky, Commonwealth of, Cabinet for Natural Resources and Environmental Protection and the Kentucky Long- Term Policy Research Center (NREPC) (1997), *Kentucky Outlook 2000: A strategy for Kentucky's third century, Executive Summary*, Frankfort, KY.

Kentucky, Commonwealth of, Cabinet for Natural Resources and Environmental Protection and the Kentucky Long- Term Policy Research Center (NREPC) (1996), *Kentucky Outlook 2000: A strategy for Kentucky's third century, Technical Reports*, Frankfort, KY.

Kentucky, Commonwealth of, Environmental Quality Commission (EQC), (1992), *State of Kentucky's Environment: A Report of Progress and Problems*, Environmental Quality Commission: Frankfort, KY.

Kentucky Long-Term Policy Research Center (LTPRC), (1995), *Visioning Kentucky's Future: Planning Strategically for the 21st Century and Measuring our Progress*, Author: Frankfort, KY.

King, D.M. (1994), 'Can We Justify Sustainability? New Challenges Facing Ecological Economics', Chapter 18, pp. 323-42 in Jansson, A., Hammer, M., Folke, C. and Constanza, R. (eds), *Investing in Natural Capital*, Island Press: Washington DC.

Krutilla, J.V. (ed.), (1972), *Natural Environments*, The Johns Hopkins University Press: Baltimore.

Lesh, D.R. and Lowrie, D.G. (1990), *Sustainable Development: A New Path for Progress*, The Global Tomorrow Coalition: Washington DC.

Lyons, T.S., Meyer, P.B. and Mani, V. (1996), 'Forecasting Kentucky's environmental futures', *Foresight: A publication of the Kentucky Long Term Policy Research Center*, Vol. 3, No. 3, pp. 1-5.

Maclaren, V.W. (1996), 'Urban Sustainability Reporting', *Journal of the American Planning Association*, Vol. LXII, No. 2, pp. 184-202.

Manning, M. and Rejeski, D. (1994), *Sustainable Development and Risk: A Fit?*, Working Paper, Future Studies Unit, U.S. Environmental Protection Agency: Washington DC.

Marshall, K. and Brown, R.S. (1995), *Jobs for a Healthy Environment/ Economy: Environmental Protection as an Economic Development Tool*, The Council of State Governments: Lexington, KY.

Mayer-Wittman, K.M. (1989), 'Economic Analysis and Corporate Strategic Planning', *Business Economics*, Vol. 24, No. 2, pp. 27-32.

McInnis, Daniel F. (1992), 'Ozone Layers and Oligopoly Profits', in Greve, Michael S. and Smith, Fred L., Jr., *Environmental Politics: Public Costs and Private Rewards*, Praeger: New York.

Mead, A. (1996), 'Dirty air may affect state economy, researchers find', *Lexington Herald-Leader*, Tuesday, July 30, pp. A4.

Meadows, D. (1972), *The Limits to Growth, A Global Challenge: a Report for the Club of Rome Project on the Predicament of Mankind*, Universe Books: New York.

Melnykovych, A. (1996), 'Kentucky's economy tied to environment', *Courier-Journal*, Louisville, July 28, pp. B1.

Meyer, P.B. (1993), *Environmental Futures and Kentucky Impacts: Some Highly Uncertain Speculations*, Center for Environmental Management, University of Louisville: Louisville, KY.

Meyer, P.B. and Lyons, T.S. (1996), *Forecasting Kentucky's Environmental Futures*, Center for Environmental Management, University of Louisville: Louisville, KY.

Meyer, S.M. (1992), *Environmentalism and Economic Prosperity: Testing the Environmental Impact Hypothesis*, Project on Environmental Politics and Policy, Massachusetts Institute of Technology: Cambridge, MA.

Milbrath, L.W. (1989), *Envisioning a Sustainable Society: Learning Our Way Out*, State University of New York Press: Albany.

Minor, R.L. (1996), 'Group's environmental outlook paints a troublesome picture', *The Daily News*, Bowling Green, October 28, pp. A2.

Mishan, E.J. (1967), *The Costs of Economic Growth*, Staples Press: London.

n.a. (1996a), 'Environmental sense: Our economy can get even better without pollution', *Lexington Herald-Leader*, July 31, pp. A2.

n.a. (1996b), 'Good air is good business', *Lexington Herald-Leader*, Monday, August 12, editorial from The Independent (Ashland), pp. A8.

n.a. (1996c), 'Green, not greed, is good', *Lexington Herald-Leader*, Sunday, December 1, editorial.

Odum, H.T. (1971), *Environment, Power, and Society*, Wiley: New York.

Opschoor, J.B. and Vos, H.B. (1995), *Economic instruments for Environmental Protection*, OECD: Paris.

Parson, E.A. (1993), 'Protecting the Ozone Layer', in Haas, P.M., Keohane, R.O. and Levy, M.A. (eds), *Institutions for the Earth*, MIT Press: Cambridge, MA.

Pearce, D.W. and Warford, J.J. (1993), *World Without End: Economics, Environment and Sustainable Development*, Oxford University Press: New York.

Perrottet, C.M. (1996), 'Scenarios for the Future', *Management Review*, Vol. 85, No. 1, pp. 43-6.

Perry, A. (1996), 'The Rise and Fall of Strategic Planning', *Business Management Practices*, Vol. 13, No. 3, pp. 275-8.

Pirages, D.C., (ed.) (1996), *Building Sustainable Societies: A Blueprint for a Post-Industrial World*, M.E. Sharpe: Armonk, NY.

Power, T.M. (1996), *Environmental Protection and Economic Well-Being: The Economic Pursuit of Quality*, M.E. Sharpe: New York.

Raskin, Paul, Sieber, Jack, Margolis, Robert and Heaps, Charles (1995), *POLESTAR System Manual: A Tool for Sustainability Studies*, Stockholm Environment Institute: Boston.

Redclift, M. (1987), *Sustainable Development:Exploring the Contradictions*, Routledge: New York.

Rejeski, D. (n.d.), *A Technology Policy for the Environment: Ten Recommendations*, Working Paper, Future Studies Unit, U.S. Environmental Protection Agency: Washington DC.

Ring, P.S. (1988), 'Strategic Issues: What Are They and From Where Do They Come?', in Bryson, J.M. and Einsweiler, R.C. (eds), *Strategic Planning: Threats and Opportunities for Planners*, American Planning Association: Chicago, IL.

Roth, P.L., Schleifer L.L.F. and Switzer, F.S. (1995), 'Nominal Group Technique: An Aid in Implementing TQM', *The CPA Journal*, Vol. 65, No. 5, 68-72.

Rowe, G. and Wright, G. (1999), 'The Delphi Technique as a Forecasting Tool: Issues and Analysis', *International Journal of Forecasting*, Vol. 15, No. 4, pp. 353-75.

Scheberle, D. (1997), *Federalism and Environmental Policy: Trust and the Politics of Implementation*, Georgetown University Press: Washington DC.

Schwartz, P. (1991), *The Art of the Long View*, Doubleday: New York.

Scruggs, P. (1995), *Seeds of Change: State Efforts Leading the Way Towards Sustainability*, Sustainability Round Table Information Forum: Portland, OR.

Selman, P. (1992), *Environmental Planning: The Conservation and Development of Biophysical Resources*, Paul Chapman Publishing: London.

Singh, H. (1990), 'Relative Evaluation of Subjective and Objective Measures of Expectations Formation', *Quarterly Review of Economics and Finance*, Vol. 30, No. 1, pp. 64-75.

Smith, Z.A. (1992), *The Environmental Policy Paradox*, Prentice Hall: Englewood Cliffs, NJ.

Smith-Mello, M., Schirmer, P. and Taylor, M.A. (1995), *Building the Capacity to Compete and Prosper*, Kentucky Long Term Policy Research Center: Frankfort, KY.

Stigliani, W.M., Brouwer, F.M., Munn, R.E., Shaw, R.W. and Antonovsky, M. (1989), *Future Environments for Europe: Some Implications of Alternative Development Paths*, International Institute for Applied Systems Analysis: Laxenburg, Austria.

United Nations (1990), *Global Outlook 2000: An Economic, Social and Environmental Perspective*, United Nations: New York.

United States, Environmental Protection Agency, Science Advisory Board, Environmental Futures Committee (EPA) (1995), *Beyond the Horizon: Using Foresight to Protect the Environmental Future*, U.S. Government Printing Office EPA-SAB-EC-95-007: Washington DC.

United States, Environmental Protection Agency, Office of Strategic Planning and Environmental Data (EPA) (1993), *Environmental Futures Project Focus Group Report: Innovative Technologies*, Washington DC.

United States, Office of the President, National Science and Technology Council (NSTC) (1994), *Technology for a Sustainable Future: a Framework for Action*, U.S. Government Printing Office: Washington DC.

United States, Whitehouse, Council on Environmental Quality (CEQ), (1997), *Considering cumulative effects under the national environmental protection act*, U.S. Government Printing Office: Washington DC [http://www.whitehouse.gov/CEO/publications].

Van den Ende, J., Mulder, K., Knot, M., Moors, E. and Vergragt, P. (1998), 'Traditional and Modern Technology Assessment: Toward a Toolkit', *Technological Forecasting and Social Change*, Vol. 58, No. 1.

Weisbuch, G., Gutowitz, H. and Duchateau-Nguyen, G. (1994), *Dynamics of Economic Choices Involving Pollution*, Laboratoire de Physique Statistique, CNRS-Universités Paris 6 et Paris 7: Paris.

Woodell, S.R.J. (1989), 'And That Was the Future: Forecasting Our Environmental Future', *Futures*, Vol. 21, No. 6, pp. 647-59.

World Commission on Environment and Development (WCED) (1987), *Our Common Future*, Oxford University Press: New York.

Appendix One:
Current trends in Kentucky

The emerging trends we used to identify relevant issues were identified through a two-year study process by the Long Term Policy Research Center (LTPRC) and published as The Context of Change (1994). Each item below summarizes a trend identified in that report. Each trend identified in that report was supported with statistical and other evidence. The section headings used here are those of the report itself and reflect public sector decision-making logic, in part mirroring the legislative committee structure of the Kentucky General Assembly. In the subsequent survey targeting environmental policy "hot spots," the thirty-seven trends were grouped differently. In that exercise, they were reordered to represent specific planning problems rather than challenges to particular institutions or policy-making bodies.

The people of Kentucky

Moderate population growth

Demographic trends suggest that Kentucky will experience only moderate population growth in the years to come, in spite of the high rate of growth it has enjoyed in the early 1990s. The stagnation of Kentucky's population during the 1980s, which is largely attributable to substantial out migration, particularly among young people, poses questions about the viability of Kentucky's future labor force.

Population homogeneity

The homogeneity of Kentucky's population has also persisted in recent years, a trend that may not bode well for the almost certain advance of globalization of commerce, which will demand high levels of comfort with diverse peoples and cultures. States that are perceived as economically or socially inhospitable to minorities may risk accelerated decline in their minority populations and thereby undermine their competitiveness.

Sustained rurality

Kentucky is expected to retain its essentially rural character for some time to come and, as a consequence, delay or avoid the arrival of some of the problems urbanization brings include congestion, crime and pollution. The beauty and the quality of life this rural strength enables may hold enormous future appeal for those in flight from urban congestion and crime.

Changing family structures

More single parented children

More children live in households headed by single parents, who are much more likely to be poor as a result of the increased incidence of divorce and a growing number of births to unmarried women.

Sharp drop in birth rate

The most pronounced factor influencing state demographics is the sharply declining birth rate. Contrary to stereotypes, Kentucky registered the second lowest birth rate in the nation during the 1980s, signaling the strong possibility of continued population decline in the state's population of young people under age 18.

More households, each with fewer members

As more of us choose to live alone and families continue to fragment, the number of households has risen while the number of people living in them has declined. While household formation continues to outpace population growth, the trend actually peaked in the 1970s. Nevertheless, the rapid expansion of households has triggered widespread, if belated, attention to the implications for families, the environment and a fraying community fabric.

Older and wiser?

Population aging

The aging of our population is the most striking population trend affecting Kentucky. This trend will persist and deepen over the first half of the 21st Century. At present it takes the form of an emerging middle-age population bulge, a decrease in the number of children and an increase in the elderly.

Expanding poverty

Because older Kentuckians are disproportionately poor, the aging of our population may be attended by expanded poverty. Rural states like Kentucky are often strained to provide much needed support services for older people, for which the demand is certain to expand.

Generations at odds

Growing conflict over intergenerational equity

Converging economic and demographic trends may worsen intergenerational tensions in the years to come. The conflicting economic and social interests of young and old are pushing the issue of generational equity higher on the public agenda in spite of the attendant political risk.

Changing economic paradigms

Demand for rising productivity

Global competition is increasing the demands on businesses and on workers. Together they have scrambled to build higher quality products, in less time and at lower cost. This seemingly limitless world marketplace is challenging firms and their employees to meet rising product and performance goals.

Information age economic shifts

The long heralded Information Age has arrived and exerted a powerful influence on the way we work and live. Technology is accelerating the rate of change and creating an explosion of opportunities for highly skilled workers and innovative firms.

A shifting economic floor

Declining coal employment due to automation, environmentalism

While Kentucky's coal industry has logged record production levels in recent years, employment in this high-wage industry has fallen sharply, largely as a consequence of technological advancements and the consolidation or closure of mine operations. Over the long term, rising environmentalism and the implementation of current and anticipated regulations complicate the utilization of Kentucky's coal reserve.

Declining tobacco-growing incomes

The future of burley tobacco, which is being influenced by declining use and increased imports of leaf, presents the most significant threat to farming and farmers in the state. In decline by several measures, including employment, farm population and cultivated land, Kentucky's farm economy nevertheless enjoys record output, as farming methods and equipment advance productivity. However, the vulnerability of its key crop, tobacco, has created significant uncertainty.

Growth in undercapitalized manufacturing firms

Predicted to decline nationally in coming years, manufacturing nevertheless is making dramatic gains in Kentucky's economy, outpacing the nation in terms of jobs and gross product. Kentucky produces a diverse range of manufacturing products; however, the predominance of small, often insufficiently capitalized firms, an inadequate base of intellectual capital, skilled workers, and technological know-how may inhibit our ability to compete in the global marketplace.

Effort to stimulate secondary wood processing

Kentucky hardwoods are prominent in the UNITED STATES marketplace. However, the absence of value-added wood products industries prevents the state from capturing the full benefit of this abundant resource. Approximately 70 to 75 per cent of the 700 million board feet of grade lumber cut annually is shipped out of state without further processing. Development of this enormous long-term economic potential will require investment in expertise, entrepreneurial initiatives, and careful attention to the cultivation of an ethic of stewardship that will help sustain this abundant resource.

Growth in historic site tourism

As our population ages, the store of historical sites in Kentucky and the state's ready accessibility are expected to increase its appeal to tourists, magnifying the economic benefit of tourism to Kentucky. While it is viewed as a viable, sustainable option for the development of rural communities, tourism is not an antidote to poverty for those holding seasonal or marginal quality jobs.

Growth in small firm demand for expertise, capital

Small enterprises are expected to be the engine of our future economy, fueled by expertise, capital and a broad-based commitment to their development. As the small-business sector of the economy continues to create the lion's share of new opportunities, the importance of enabling entrepreneurs rises. Much of the state's future success in cultivating small enterprises and the opportunities they will yield hinges on the availability of expertise (managerial and technical) and capital.

Chasing the dream

Growing instability of employment

Increasingly, the notion of lifetime employment is now widely viewed as an anachronism, and hard work is no longer an assurance of anything. For many workers, the American Dream has become more elusive and the pursuit of it a frantic chase. The employer-employee contract is becoming more tenuous, as firms meet global competition with fewer, less costly employees, many of whom work part-time or on a contingency basis. Wages have stagnated and, at the same time, employee benefit packages are shrinking or disappearing.

Growing proportions of working poor households

The percentage of poor working families in Kentucky grew during the 1980s and continued to exceed that of the nation as whole. Rising levels of contingency employment, the ascendance of low-wage industries, a reciprocal decline in high-wage industries, low labor force participation, and the types and the mix of jobs that industry is bringing to the state influence wage levels.

Increasing income inequality within Kentucky

In Kentucky, income inequality became more pronounced over the most recent decade. Increasingly, economists view deepening disadvantage as a problem with broad-based implications. Falling UNITED STATES wages have been accompanied by the rise of income inequality and what many analysts believe is a shrinking middle class. The impoverishment and decline that inequality fosters is believed to discourage investment and, in turn, adversely affect productivity.

Growing potential for worker-management conflict

The importance of forging joint worker-manager efforts to address emerging problems is rising on the policy making landscape. As more workers face growing uncertainty fueled by stagnant wages, diminishing benefits, continued layoffs, and the prospect of rising workloads and work hours, the critical relationship between worker and employer is being undermined.

Fiscal health

Continued centrality of state revenue collection

Kentucky's fiscal structure is characterized by a heavy concentration of taxing and spending at the state level, more so than in other states. Consequently, the people of Kentucky rely heavily on state government to provide services, financing, infrastructure and leadership on matters that are traditionally the obligations or prerogatives of local governments in other states.

Growing local, county fiscal stress

In recent years, the burden placed on city and county budgets by unfunded federal mandates has received particular scrutiny in recent years. These mandates are exerting increasing fiscal pressure on local governments. Despite the concentration of fiscal responsibilities at the state level, the finances of counties, cities and special districts are extremely important. Local governments are responsible for a quarter of total state and local expenditures in Kentucky.

Transportation

Emergence of new transportation modes

A number of forces now at work will expand the role of other modes of transportation and dramatically alter the transportation planning process. A quality transportation system will be critical to Kentucky's future prosperity. Highways, the quality of which is improving even as use expands, are the traditional backbone of this system, and they will continue to be so in coming years. Federal legislation, environmental considerations, competition for business and technological advances will affect the modes chosen to deliver needed services in the future.

Environmental integrity

New efforts to prevent water pollution

The quality of Kentucky's water continues to improve, but substantial investment in infrastructure will be required in coming years, to safely treat wastewater and extend public drinking water to more Kentuckians. New approaches to managing pollution are likely to focus on the source, rather than the outcome, of water pollution.

Shift in demand for coal due to Clean Air Act Amendments of 1990

Kentucky's air quality has improved dramatically since the enactment of the federal Clean Air Act in 1970, the provisions of which have led to significant reductions in levels of harmful pollutants, such as lead and carbon monoxide. When fully enforced, the federal Clean Air Act Amendments of 1990 are expected to dramatically reduce air pollution, but they will have an as yet undetermined impact on the state's coal industry.

Rising landfill costs, new pressures to recycle

Programs to promote waste reduction and recycling will likely increase, as landfill disposal costs rise and more markets for recyclables become available. Timely legislation has checked the influx of out-of-state garbage, but management of Kentucky's solid waste continues to challenge policy makers at every level.

New prescriptions for health care

Growth in health promotion/disease prevention efforts

Health care emphasis is shifting to health promotion and disease prevention as a means of making health care more accessible and affordable while retaining quality. A higher level of cooperation among individuals, private service providers and government is expected to emerge as well. Advanced applications of technology and more active involvement of communities will overarch these trends, as we attempt to create a more manageable, useful and equitable health care system.

A future imperiled by poverty

Continued high childhood poverty rates

From one-fourth to nearly one-half of Kentucky's children live in poverty. Research has consistently confirmed that poverty adversely affects the health and educational attainment of children. In turn, these effects translate into adverse effects on the productivity and independence of their adult lives.

Toward lifelong learning

Increasing demands for adult education and training

By virtually every measure, Kentuckians are undereducated and ill prepared to meet the challenges of the future. Prominent among the deficiencies are high dropout rates, a low rate of college attendance and one of the highest rates nationally of adults with less than high school completion. While significant progress is being made, Kentucky still has far to go in its drive to close persistent education and training deficits.

Continued financial demands to implement KERA

The Kentucky Education Reform Act has yielded measurable improvements in the performance of students. As well, it has engaged thousands of parents, teachers and administrators in a new way of thinking about education. In spite of its ranking at or near the bottom of the fifty states in many aspects of educational attainment, Kentucky has ascended to national prominence in educational reform.

Growth in pre-employment, non-college training

By the turn of the Century, the majority of UNITED STATES workers will need more than a high school diploma. Increasingly, educational need has extended beyond the basics provided by a high school education. As the demand for highly trained workers who have a solid intellectual foundation continues to expand, the importance of honing the skills of new and current workers is critical.

Relative decline in University funding

While higher education continues to provide the intellectual capital needed to meet future challenges, cost poses an increasingly formidable obstacle to its benefits. Knowledge and the analytical and creative skills higher education enables are becoming central to our lives. Unfortunately, competing and compelling needs have eroded once generous public funding for higher education, challenging administrators to do more with fewer state dollars and prompting closer scrutiny at every level.

Responding to crime

Rising juvenile crime

Data on violent crime suggest it may be rising in Kentucky. At the same time, however, Kentucky's crime rate is quite low and only a fraction of regional (South) and national crime rates.

Rising juvenile arrests

Juvenile arrests for serious offenses have also risen in Kentucky.

Rising prison populations

Predictably, prison populations have risen accordingly. Over the past 20 years, the rate of incarceration has increased 233 percent in Kentucky. The rising costs associated with increased incarceration are challenging policy makers to discover and implement alternatives to prison. As an important starting point, Kentucky's criminal justice system has begun to explore mediation as an alternative to litigation and to shift nonviolent offenders to less costly facilities or to home incarceration.

Building social capital

Need to raise community participation, involvement

While hopeful signs of rising engagement can be detected in the civic life of Kentucky, many community activists observe that, for a variety of reasons, civic engagement is inadequate and, therefore, self-limiting. Despite this, government must, as a matter of routine, turn to citizens for guidance, direction and support, if it hopes to build the social capital on which successful development relies. The effectiveness of government in the future will depend upon the ability of its leaders to overcome cynicism, alienation and even despair among the citizens it serves and build the social capital or citizen participation needed to meet the challenges before us. Research shows that those communities and regions that enjoy high levels of civic engagement are far more prosperous.

List of acronyms

BSQ   Baseline Status Quo scenario
CH4   Methane
CO2   Carbon dioxide
EPA   United States Environmental Protection Agency
GDP   Gross domestic product
LTPRC Kentucky Long Term Policy Research Center
KIESD Kentucky Institute for the Environment and Sustainable
         Development
PCS   Policy Change Scenario
RCC   Restructured Combined Change scenario
SO2   Sulfur dioxide
TCS   Technological Change Scenario
TSP   Total Suspended Particulates
U.S.   United States
VOC   Volatile Organic Compounds

Note: acronyms used in citations are listed in the bibliography